contributions in sociology 3

Don Martindale

Department of Sociology, University of Minnesota

R. Galen Hanson

Department of Sociology, Normandale State College

SMALL TOWN AND THE NATION

THE CONFLICT OF LOCAL AND TRANSLOCAL FORCES

Greenwood Publishing Corporation

Westport, Connecticut

Library of Congress Catalog Card Number: 79–90793
SBN: 8371–4991–6

Greenwood Publishing Corporation
51 Riverside Avenue, Westport, Conn. 06880
Greenwood Publishers Ltd., 42 Hanway Street, London, W1, England
Printed in the United States of America

Designed by Joan Stoliar

For the People of Benson

CONTENTS

THE CONFRONTATIONS OF
POWER AND INFLUENCE **8** 148

SMALL TOWN AND THE NATION

TABLES

List of Tables

PREFACE

As wave upon wave of migrants from the eastern seaboard, the South, and from Europe swept west across
continental America in the nineteenth century, thousands of
towns and cities sprang up to service them. The dominant
tradition of these budding communities was that of the self-
sufficient New England town. Each developed all the institutions necessary for the full life of its citizens: a government, religious institutions, schools, a variety of economic

institutions, etc. The traditions of town-meeting democracy were powerful among their members: they ran their own affairs; they took care of their own problems. And well into the 1890's they experienced themselves as firm vertebrae ("backbone" as they put it) of an America that still primarily had the character of a great loose federation of small towns and cities.

However, even by this time great urban concentrations of population were forming. The rise of mass industry accelerated after the Civil War. The forms of mass transportation were destroying the sheer physical isolation of local life while men by the millions were beginning to buy and sell in continent-wide markets. The effective points of gravity were relocating in emerging mass industries, in the great metropolitan centers, in the state and federal rather than in local political institutions. Hence, slowly at first but accelerating in time, small towns and cities began to lose ground and in many hundreds of cases to vanish altogether.

In the twentieth-century world the Jeffersonian ideal of autonomous small towns has become anachronistic. Power is shifting from the locality to the great centers of government, industry, and finance. If the small town survives at all it is not as an autonomous center of local life but as a semidependent agency of distant power centers.

Much of the drama of local life in the twentieth century lies in the clash of the old ideals of the autonomous community with the realities of survival in a mass world. The manner in which impulses arising from these two sources appear in conflict and are resolved is the primary object of this study of Benson, a small town of some 4,000 people in west-central Minnesota.

Benson's crisis is assumed to arise from the clash of old ideals with contemporary realities. It was hypothesized that the conflict of forces is present in all major areas of Benson's institutional life.

I. The lines of tension between local and nonlocal forces are discernible in the economy of Benson.

II. Benson's structure of power and influence is polarized in terms of local and nonlocal interests.

III. The major lines of stress in Benson's institutions of socialization arise from the conflict of local and non-local interests.

Data for testing these hypotheses were gathered by participant observation, by a perusal of numerous documentary and published sources, by extensive interviewing and an analytical survey of samples of Bensonites and ex-Bensonites. A questionnaire was designed covering a variety of social characteristics and attitudes theorized to be relevant to the clash between localism and translocalism. This questionnaire was carefully checked for reliability, validity, and organized into scales of localism (orientation toward the goal of local community autonomy) and cosmopolitanism (orientation toward extracommunity forces). Two samples of Bensonites were set up: old-style Bensonites (persons who were theorized to be traditional in orientation) and new-style Bensonites (persons who were anticipated to transmit the translocal forces). Systematic predictions of differences could then be made as to findings with respect to the two groups. The sample of ex-Bensonites was drawn primarily as a control group. It was theorized that in some respects they should differ from either of the Bensonite samples: in origin they were similar to old-style Bensonites; however, since they had left Benson to make their way in the wider world, they should resemble in attitudes the new-style Bensonites.

Each item of the questionnaire, thus, became a working test of one or other of the general hypotheses. The data were processed through the computers, and chi-square tests of significance were calculated with respect to findings on the various samples. With some minor exceptions the working hypotheses were verified. The general hypotheses were confirmed beyond question.

In our attempt to gain insight into Benson, we have drawn deeply upon the wisdom and knowledge of Mr. and Mrs. Russell Hanson, the parents of the junior author, and upon that of his brother, Burton Randall Hanson. It is difficult to express here all we owe them. We are obliged to Edith Martindale for checking many of our statistical computations. The board and staff members of the Swift County Historical Society and of the Benson Public Library were most cooperative and went out of their way to make historical material available to us. We also owe a debt of gratitude to the officials of various Benson institutions for making available to us a variety of organizational reports and records. Special thanks are due to those Bensonites and ex-Bensonites who generously gave of their time to be interviewed, and to respond to the questionnaire so essential to the quantitative aspects of our study.

We were met with such a general spirit of friendly cooperation that we must express our thanks to the people of Benson: this is their story.

Don Martindale
R. Galen Hanson

February, 1969

SMALL TOWN AND THE NATION

1

THE
SMALL
TOWN
IN A
MASS
WORLD

Driving west on U.S. Highway 12 on a summer day, the motorist, as he approaches the South Dakota border, becomes aware of the fact that he is in the transition area where Minnesota's forest region melts into the Great Plains. Forested areas recede in importance, the number of streams and lakes declines, the land loses its relief and flattens toward the great upland plain. It is an area where great prairie fires once swept in off the plains to thrust back the encroaching forests. One need only close one's eyes to envision the buffalo that once roamed the area and see the land as the far eastern range of the grizzly bear.

White settlement brought drastic changes. The Indians were displaced. Control measures of various kinds halted the prairie fires. The great bear were killed. The buffalo vanished. Fire protection and careful cultivation encouraged nuclei of forest and wood-lot growth, alternating with prosperous farms. But the atmosphere still retains a dry, light quality, like a half-lost memory of the great upland plains that once claimed the area. And the motorist in response to this subtle change of atmosphere may be inclined to stop at Benson, to purchase a Coke at Norsk's Bakery-Café, to stretch his legs, and saunter about a small-town crossroad that he might otherwise pass through with hardly any notice.

Should our hypothetical motorist gaze about the center of Benson, it is quite possible that one of the first structures he would see would be the Swift County courthouse. Our sojourner might possibly be amused by the slightly pretentious air of authority of the building, like the proud, inappropriate self-importance of a member of an old family whose fortunes had tarnished somewhat with age. And if our observer turns from this image of bygone grandeur, he may experience another mild surprise. For directly across the square from the Swift County courthouse is another structure, the Park View Manor, as distinctive for its streamlined modernity as is the courthouse for its traditionalism. In this architectural contrast of traditional and modern styles

2

in Benson's town square, two competing ways of life meet in direct confrontation. In the studies of the small community by American social scientists since the 1920s, this confrontation has gradually moved into central focus.

THE PLACE OF THE SMALL
TOWN IN A MASS WORLD

Benson, Minnesota, is a small town with a population of approximately 4,000. It is similar to thousands of small towns that not long ago typified American life and that, to the deep concern of some observers, have been losing ground and disappearing by the hundreds before other forces of American life. Studies of the small town since the 1920s have brought the conflict of local and translocal forces ever more clearly into perspective.

Tipton

In his 1928 study of the small town of Tipton, J. F. Steiner characterized the social cohesion of the small community as a loyalty and unity that endures in spite of disintegrating forces from the outside.[1] At this time, the majority of sociologists still conceived the essential America as the world of the small town. Though, like Steiner, many were growing increasingly aware that the outside forces were beginning to press upon the small town, it remained the basis for their hopes. Thus, although the Great Depression shook large city and small town alike, thousands returned to the small towns to weather the storm. Then World War II set industry into high gear, particularly in the large urban-industrial areas, sucking the working population out of the small towns into its service. When World War II was over and the labor and soldier populations, if so inclined, considered return, there was often no small town left to return to. In the postwar period the balance between internal and external forces in the small town has tipped in favor of the latter.

Plainville

James West's study of Plainville in 1945 was oriented to the notion that disintegrating forces from the outside do, in fact, disturb the equilibrium of the small town. Pressures from the outside operate with special power on the educational system. West reported that the parents of Plainville wished to keep their children in Plainville and effectively restricted their chances for success by the very nature of Plainville's schools.[2]

> Everybody realizes that many children must leave, or "will want to leave," yet each parent hopes that his own children will not be among the "ones to go." No effort is made to prepare any children for life beyond Plainville in any capacity except as day laborers, since school teachers do not dare to encroach on territory regarding which parents have such strong feelings, and reformers concern themselves only with alleviating or improving local conditions. When families were much larger, and land claims

4

were free in the West, parents were apparently better adjusted to the migration of children. Children were then only repeating a pattern familiar to all farm parents, but children who migrate to cities are frequently considered "lost" in more ways than one. The hostility to "new ideas" and to "higher education" and the stressing in churches of the "sins of the cities" are devices by which, whatever their other functions, parents strive to keep their children in Plainville, and effectively restrict their success when they leave.[3]

Though its children are Plainville's most vital export, their success is seriously restricted by the socialization process in their formative years in Plainville.

The "outside world" absorbs about one-half of all of Plainville's children. But West found that *neither* reformers (who ask for change in Plainville's schools), nor schools, nor parents in Plainville deal realistically with the fact (though reformers understand the basic truth of the fact) that Plainville produces *more* children than it can accommodate permanently.[4]

West's analysis of Plainville was by no means concerned only with the destiny of its excess children, but primarily with its self-maintenance. West found that in Plainville knowledge and power were locked into a closed system. Plainville's network of informal power was sustained *both* by rigidly restrictive knowledge of everyone *and* by euphemistic proclamations of equality. Almost from the first, the Plainville citizen gained a catalog of information about everyone in town with special pigeonholes for every person. The categories are rigid, and once recognized, for example, as one of the "Jones boys," an individual finds it hard to climb out of his niche. Despite their system of interlocked inequalities, the Plainvillites affirm the equality of all.

> The class system of Plainville might well be called a "super organization," because it provides for every person living there a master pattern for arranging according to relative rank every other individual, and every family, clique, lodge, club, church, and other organization and association in Plainville society. . . . Yet, many, if not most, Plainvillers completely deny the existence of class in the community. . . . About Plainville and most of Woodland County they often say with some pride, "There is one place where ever'body is equal. You don't find no classes here."[5]

The system of interlocked individual inequalities is protected by the credo of the democratic equalitarianism of the group. The forces for local autonomy thus are demonstrated to operate negatively to progressive forces from the outside and are deleterious to the life chances of those young persons forced to migrate.

Jonesville

Warner's analysis of Jonesville in 1949 was also directed to the self-maintenance of the small town in a wider world. Its hierarchy of power comprised "squire farmers," "old landowners," "dirt farmers," and "lower-lowers," reflecting both the rural world the small town serves and the wide urban world to which it responds. The "squire farmers" were landowning members of old families with reputations as outstanding persons, who have acquired high-status, urban culture patterns. "Old landowners" are similar but lack-

6

ing in the urban culture patterns possessed by the "squires." "Dirt farmers" are not from old families and chiefly find their occupational identity as tenant farmers and hired hands, though a few own small farms of their own. "Lower-lowers," who drifted from tenant farm to tenant farm, occupied the base of the hierarchy in Jonesville.[6]

The class structure was found to be relatively rigid. Upward mobility from "dirt farmer" to "old landowner" posed especially difficult problems.[7] While the power of the upper status group rested on its position as top of the local hierarchy, its style of life reflected the urban world outside. One could anticipate the potential collapse of the local system should representatives of the urban world arrive on the scene.

Springdale

By and large, the studies of the small town in the 1960s are directed to its transformation or decline under the influence of the wider society. Vidich and Bensman find the key to power in the small town in the political broker who is "dependent on the businessmen since they constitute an important part of his legal clientele and since he receives fees from public funds which they administrate, but this does not mean that he is an errand boy."[8] The most powerful single person in Springdale was found to be a shy, quiet, unassuming man who never appeared to stand out in public situations but who, in fact, exerted more power than any other person in town.[9] "Everyone in the community knows that Jones is the most powerful man in town and that he is the political boss, but only a few can deal with him directly as a political boss. His personality reinforces his unapproachability."[10] Jones attained his position by an informal, behind-the-scenes, anonymous style of operation.[11]

Springdale was found to be dependent on the institutions of urban mass society. Springdale's people were in awe of the mass world. But Springdale's people also know that local life is devalued by the urban world outside and their respect for the mass society is tempered with resentment.[12]

While Springdale, thus, has its own center of power, its local governing institutions are so dominated by the institutions of the metropolis that its officials find it difficult to act even in those areas where they have jurisdiction.[13]

Vandalia

Joseph Lyford goes further in his observations on the relation of local and translocal forces, portraying the small town as subordinated to the superstructure of the mass society. In *The Talk in Vandalia,* the very survival of the small town is questioned. The small town is depicted by Lyford as a small social unit engaged in a desperate, daily battle for economic survival. Vandalia's families were found to be uncertain about their future and the future of their community. To be sure, rosy employment statistics were turned out by Vandalia's chamber of commerce in its brochures, but in fact jobs in Vandalia were vanishing, on Main Street, on the farms, and in the factories. The great proportion of

8

available jobs could not support a family nor did they offer much hope for social-economic advancements.

> The family that wants to remain in Vandalia, far from being insulated from the tensions and threats of the outer world, is resisting economic, social, and technological forces that could break the community apart and send the pieces flying in all directions.[14]

Even on a Sunday morning amidst a church service, Vandalia's quiet air is pierced as the crack passenger train, symbol of the great world outside, streaks through town. "Judge Burnside says nobody pays any attention to the railroads. On the other hand, in his church by the railroad, Mr. Smith has to stop in the middle of his Sunday sermon when he hears the 'Spirit of Saint Louis' coming down the tracks."[15]

New Ulm

While Noel Iverson's study of New Ulm, Minnesota, was not directly concerned with local versus translocal forces, it was directed to certain historical changes in a small town under the conditions of the wider society, which in part reflect them.[16] Iverson traced the change of the most wealthy and powerful group of the city in its transition from an ethnic into a status group, a change responsive to conditions in the wider society.[17]

Originally, political leadership had been consolidated in the hands of members of the German *Turnverein,* who established an isolated socialistic community. But by the second generation, leadership was channeled in part into

9

other sectors of the community as well, even though the *Turners* continued to exert an important role.[18] At an early period the *Turners* had found it profitable to drop their utopian community experiment and to convert themselves into a business and political elite serving other later-arrived immigrants. They consolidated their initial leadership position into a traditional role, exerting significant influence on civic affairs in their town and in the state. Soon after the 1860s, newly arrived settlers outnumbered the *Turners* ten to one, and some of their members began to rise to leadership positions on their own. The historical and cultural experiences of the founders accounted for their initial formation as an ethnic community; the forces of the outside world transformed their community and led them to the consolidation of their new position as upper status elite.[19] The small town of New Ulm was changing in response to autonomous forces and forces arising in the wider society.

The Small Town in Perspective

In the 1920s and 1930s, the small town was still being viewed by the social scientists who studied it as the permanent unchallengeable heart of American life. In the 1930s and 1940s, studies of the small town increasingly viewed it as tending to glide outside the mainstream of American life, though they rarely questioned its capacity to survive or its intrinsic importance. In the 1950s and 1960s the changes in the small town (New Ulm), the problem of its survival (Vandalia) in a mass world, and even of its very significance (Springdale) have increasingly dominated social science analysis.

10

THE RESOURCES OF CONTEMPORARY
COMMUNITY THEORY

The small town is a type of community that by general agreement is embattled in the current world. The decline in importance of the small town is one of the primary reasons for the judgment by some sociologists that the community itself is going into eclipse.[20] Other sociologists have interpreted the same phenomena as requiring a revision of the entire community concept to update its application to contemporary conditions. This has led to the reanalysis of the principles and processes of community formation. The conceptual resources of these new developments in community theory will be drawn upon for the explanation of the internal tensions of the small town of Benson.

The most general change in the theory of community is the reevaluation of the importance of locality for community. Older and newer concepts of community can be distinguished: the first emphasizes the importance of territorial anchorage of community; the second reduces territory to a secondary (even at times dispensable) attribute of community, emphasizing, rather, the unity of the system of common life. Thinkers insisting on the essentiality of territory are inclined to conceive the community as disappearing; thinkers regarding territory as nonessential, on the other hand, continue to view "community" as a major concept of contemporary sociology.

11

Antecedents: "Community" Concepts

The notion of "community" as a unity of institutions anchored in territory was originally most incisively advanced by Henry Sumner Maine, a social theorist and student of comparative jurisprudence. Maine envisioned social development as a historical progression from the ancient village community to the modern city, in which social life underwent radical reconstruction from a system of relationships based on kinship to a more complex and more differentiated *legal* order based on contract and territory.[21]

Ferdinand Toennies recast Maine's notion of evolutionary development of community forms into the famous *Gemeinschaft-Gesellschaft* typology. *Gemeinschaft* referred to a community anchored in the natural will (feeling and sentiment), *Gesellschaft* to a community anchored in the rational will (conscious arrangements). Thus Toennies, while picking up Maine's territorially based community concept, added the notion of differential social psychologies.[22] Territorial location and life-style became two predominant threads in social science conceptualizations of the community.

Decline of the Territorial Principle

The notion of community as a territorial formation, however, proved to be an obstacle to optimum research on the community. In C. J. Galpin's study of rural Wisconsin service centers, the territorial principle did not provide effective bases for analysis. Galpin soon discovered that if he were to account for the actualities of social life he had

12

to abandon the notion of territorial entities. When he charted the limits and distributions of services (paper routes, shopping centers, milk routes), he discovered that social phenomena of rural Wisconsin were vastly complicated and the boundaries far more blurred than the territorial principles suggested.[23]

Galpin's virtual abandonment of a territorial principle sent shock waves through "community theory." In light of Galpin's findings, the theory of community has developed along two avenues, which may be ideally depicted by the contrasts in conceptualization between Robert E. Park, Ernest W. Burgess, and Roderick McKenzie on the one hand, and R. M. MacIver and E. C. Lindeman on the other. The former stressed a social ecological approach to community, while the latter stressed a network of common meanings and values that need not necessarily be limited territorially.[24]

Meanwhile developments in communication and transportation were ripping social relations loose from their territorial moorings. However, social life did not thereby lose its unity: it acquired a new viability.[25] The form of theorizing which stressed common meanings and values rather than spatial location was relevant to these trends.

Community Formation

The approach to community of the present study takes the common system of social life, not physical locus or spatial relations, as the essence of community, though the older territorial concept remains a subcategory of community. As a systematic unity of life, the community comprises a system of groups and institutions sufficient to enable the membership to survive the trials of an average year and an average life.[26]

Institutions are the patterned responses of pluralities of persons to common problems.[27] The survival of human groups depends on the efficacy of their institutions, their solutions to three general problems of social life: socialization, the mastery of nature, and social control.[28] The theory of community, with its concern with the more comprehensive patterns of social life, is specifically addressed to interadjustment of the institutions of one area of social life to influences arising out of another.[29] Such interadjustments lead, ultimately, to some stabilizing not only of the solutions to particular problems but to their interrelation into a distinctive way of life. Three general empirical processes—stabilization, consistency, and completeness—act to establish any given community as a distinct way of life.

The Stabilization of Problem Solutions

The stabilization of solutions to collective problems has peculiarities for human pluralities. Since man has few or at most rudimentary instincts, he is faced with the alternatives either of inventing his own solutions to life's problems or of learning them from other people. Institutions are the tested solutions of a socially transmitted "survival kit." Once acquired, institutions release man from the necessity of finding new solutions to old problems every time there is a turnover in generations. Established ways of dealing with problems are cemented into habits and customs. "The first step toward community formation is the stabilization of the solutions to collective problems."[30]

Interproblem Adjustments

With the emergence of stable patterns of behavior, actions congruent with them are favored over actions incongruent with them. Inevitably there is some necessity to adjust to one another the institutions formed in the several spheres of social life, the political, the economic, the religious, etc. The failure of such accommodation may cause tensions between various sectors of behavior. For example, incongruence between the business and educational institutions of a plurality, wherein each offers to the community a different solution to a specific problem, will normally have to be solved in favor of one or the other or some compromise between the two, or much waste of effort may result. In any case, there is a force toward transinstitutional consistency. Human life tends to become stylized across its separate spheres.

Institutional Completeness

But in the reworking of solutions to problems to fit them to one another the original solution may be impaired. There is a question as to how far the process of interadjustment tends to go. A plurality needs to come to grips with the problem of the full yearly cycle, and the full life cycle. Once a group of persons can get through one year and one lifetime, the set of problems-encounters repeats. Hence it is only necessary to develop a set of institutions complete enough to carry the plurality through all major tasks of

15

socialization, mastery of nature, and social control. Completion refers to the stylization by which the institutions of a plurality are cycled to carry the modal man through the course of a modal year and modal life.[31]

THE CRISIS OF BENSON

The theory and principles of community formation go far toward explaining the origin and development of Benson and its current tensions. Benson, Minnesota, was founded by Norwegian immigrants, dreaming of a better life on the frontier of the New World. Its economy was established by hardworking, thrifty peasant farmers. They had products to market and purchases to make; hence they were not long in adding various service and supply businesses to their emerging community. They had health needs to care for and children to rear, political objectives to promote, and legal snarls to untangle. The Benson, Minnesota, represented by the old county courthouse was the product of the principles of stabilization, interinstitutional consistency, and completeness, as these immigrants attempted to form an autonomous local way of life. Doctor Scofield would do what he could for a patient; the county government established the political and legal framework necessary for county life throughout the year; a network of rural schools flourished around the county and was governed by school boards elected in many small and distinct school districts and watched over by the county school superintendent elected in county-wide elections; and all of these institutions achieved a kind of sealed-off sufficiency. Benson, in short, emerged as one of the largely self-sufficient small towns that grew up by the thousands as the nuclei of local life on the American frontier.

However, while there were significant forces inclining Benson to form a close-knit autonomous local unit, there were others that ran counter to such self-sufficiency. From the beginning Bensonites envisioned the need to export their farm products to the outside and to import a wide variety of manufactured products. For this reason they were concerned with transportation facilities that gave them access to outside markets. They were, moreover, faced with the financing of their farms and businesses and concerned with access to the money and credit facilities of the wider society. Moreover, it early became evident that they were rearing more children than their community could absorb; they had to train their children for survival not only in Benson but, to some extent, in the wider world outside. Hence the drive toward local self-sufficiency could never become a completely exclusive one. Nevertheless, throughout the nineteenth century it is not unfair to estimate that the drive toward local self-sufficiency outweighed the counter-forces thereto.

However, the world outside Benson was also changing. America in the post–Civil War period was in transition from a nation of federated small towns to a national world of megalopolitan complexes that gobbled up town, countryside, and city alike. In the American Midwest these new forces became predominant in the twentieth century, particularly in the period after World War I. Before this onslaught, many a small town declined, sometimes even was turned into a ghost town. But if, at this stage, the contribution of the locality to the wider community was significant enough, new institutions might appear: grain elevators, headquarters of a marketing cooperative, REA office, a federal or state experiment station, office of the state or federal forestry or wildlife service, etc. Perhaps, if the local labor supply warranted it, a manufacturing plant might be established to take advantage of a favorable tax situation and available supply of cheap labor. Or again a state or federal medical institution might find it to be a favorable site.

The appearance of such institutions of the wider society is often welcomed with mixed feelings on the local scene. While on the one hand they stay the decline of local life, bringing new faces and new payrolls to enliven social life and spark the local economy, they also corrode the local synthesis of institutions. The point of synthesis of these new institutions lies outside the local community.

All of this has a bearing on the crisis of Benson, which is a version of the general crisis of the small town in American society. Our major hypothesis is that the small town in the mass world is internally torn by the conflict of local and translocal forces.

Derivation of Subhypotheses

From our major hypothesis, that two systems of community formation, the local and the national, establish the primary lines of cleavage in Benson's social life, three major sub-hypotheses are derived:

   I. The lines of tension between local and nonlocal forces are discernible in the economy of Benson.

  II. Benson's structure of power and influence is polarized in terms of local and nonlocal interests.

 III. The major lines of stress in Benson's institutions of socialization arise from the conflict of local and nonlocal interests.

NOTES

1. J. F. Steiner, *The American Community in Action* (New York: Henry Holt, 1928), p. 358.

2. James West, *Plainville, U.S.A.* (New York: Columbia University Press, 1945), p. 220.

3. *Ibid.,* pp. 219–220.

4. *Ibid.,* p. 219.

5. *Ibid.,* p. 115.

6. W. Lloyd Warner, *Democracy in Jonesville* (New York: Harper and Brothers, 1949), pp. 245–250.

7. *Ibid.,* p. 251.

8. Arthur J. Vidich and Joseph Bensman, *Small Town in Mass Society* (New York: Doubleday Anchor Books, 1960), p. 279.

9. *Ibid.,* pp. 281–282.

10. *Ibid.,* pp. 281–282.

11. *Ibid.,* p. 282.

12. *Ibid.,* p. 102.

13. *Ibid.,* p. 101.

14. Joseph P. Lyford, *The Talk in Vandalia* (Charlotte, N. C.: McNally and Loftin, 1962), p. 128.

15. *Ibid.,* p. 132.

16. Noel Iverson, "Germania, U.S.A.: The Dynamics of Change of an Ethnic Community into a Status Community" (Ph.D. diss., University of Minnesota, 1964).

17. *Ibid.,* p. 200.

18. *Ibid.,* p. 200.

19. *Ibid.,* pp. 202–205.

20. See Maurice R. Stein, *The Eclipse of Community* (Princeton, N.J.: Princeton University Press, 1960).

21. Henry Sumner Maine, *Ancient Law* (New York: Henry Holt, 1906).

22. Ferdinand Toennies, *Gemeinschaft und Gesellschaft* (Leipzig: K. Curtius, 1887).

23. C. J. Galpin, *The Social Anatomy of an Agricultural Village* (Madison, Wis.: Agricultural Experiment Station of the University of Wisconsin, Research Bulletin, No. 34, May, 1915), pp. 2–5.

24. Robert E. Park, Ernest W. Burgess, and Roderick McKenzie, *The City* (Chicago: University of Chicago Press, 1925). R. M. MacIver, *Community* (New York: Macmillan, 1917). E. C.

SMALL TOWN AND THE NATION

Lindeman, "Community," in *Encyclopedia of the Social Sciences* (New York: Macmillan, 1934).

25.   Don Martindale, *American Social Structure* (New York: Appleton-Century-Crofts, 1960), pp. 132–133, 147–149.

26.   Don Martindale, *Social Life and Cultural Change* (New York: D. Van Nostrand and Co., 1962), p. 44.

27.   Martindale, *American Social Structure,* p. 306.

28.   Don Martindale, *American Society* (New York: D. Van Nostrand and Co., 1960), pp. 254–255. *See also* Martindale, *Social Life and Cultural Change,* pp. 39–44.

29.   *Ibid.,* p. 44.

30.   Martindale, *American Society,* p. 108.

31.   Martindale, *Social Life and Cultural Change,* pp. 45–46.

2

THE
PHYSICAL
AND
CULTURAL
SETTING

A little over one hundred years ago, west-central Minnesota was disputed territory of the Chippewa and the Sioux Indians. Wandering hunters and raiders of both tribes came into conflict over this flat prairie of tall grass and abundant small lakes and sloughs. The physical resources of the area were rich and varied.

PHYSICAL RESOURCES
AND GEOGRAPHY

Rivers

Two rivers traversed west-central Minnesota: the Pomme de Terre and the Chippewa. The Pomme de Terre rises in Grant County and flows through the western part of Swift, past Appleton, into the Minnesota River. The largest of the numerous streams and creeks of the Pomme de Terre drain Lake Griffin in the northwest corner of the county. The Pomme de Terre valley is a mile wide near the upper boundary of the county, spreading out into a lowland several miles in width as it nears the Minnesota. This fall of forty-four feet was early put to use by the pioneers to grind their flour and feed.[1]

Charles Cooley theorized that communities have often tended to emerge between breaking points in transportation routes, such as rivers. In Swift County, the settlements of Benson and Appleton and Swift Falls are cases in point.

The Chippewa courses through the middle of Swift County and into the Minnesota River. The southeastern portion is drained by the Chippewa as it is joined by the Shakopee Creek in Swenoda township. The Little Chippewa, called also East Branch, joins the Chippewa in Benson township and drains the northeastern part of the county. One mill was built near section three of Camp Lake township, which had a head of eleven feet and could have been

23

increased to twenty-two feet by digging a canal and moving its locus one fifth of a mile farther downstream. For several miles along the Chippewa in the townships of Clontarf, Six Mile Grove, and Swenoda, appears a large flat area one to two miles in width and only ten to twenty feet above the river. An abundant water and power supply was available to potential settlers.[2]

Besides two rivers, west-central Minnesota was richly provided with numerous small lakes and sloughs. So ample was the water supply available to the early settlers that in many places the wells did not have to be dug more than twenty-two feet to reach water.[3]

Relief

In their comprehensive study of the geology of Minnesota, N. H. Winchell and Warren Upham, state the comparative elevations of selected sectors of Swift County, including Benson (Table 1). The elevations and depressions vary from ten to thirty feet, constituting long, smooth slopes rather than sharp differences. The highest elevations are in Kerkhoven, whose "massive" hills extend about one hundred feet above the plain. In the immediate vicinity of Benson township, the overwhelming impression given the eye by this topography is that of gently contoured prairie.

Soil

The soil of the Benson area is clay blended with sand and gravel, having its upper one or two feet blackened by decaying vegetation. This black soil gradually changes to a

24

TABLE 1

RELIEF OF SWIFT COUNTY

AREA	Water Grade	Elevation
Shakopee Creek	1,084	1,090
Kerkhoven		1,108
DeGraff		1,061
Benson		1,047
Chippewa River	1,035	1,035
Clontarf		1,044
Appleton		1,077
Pomme de Terre	978	1,007
Line between Swift and		
Big Stone counties		987

Source: N. H. Winchell and Warren Upham, *The Geology of Minnesota* (Saint Paul: St. Paul Pioneer Press Co., 1884–1901), vol. 2, chap. 7, ser. 6, plate 39, pp. 208–209.

substrata of yellowish till, and after ten to twenty feet to a dark blue-black. Limestone contributes to its fertility. In some areas near Benson, clay of a quality sufficient for making bricks has been located. In the 1870s, several acres of land in nearby DeGraff were so used. In 1877 alone, 300,000 bricks were manufactured in DeGraff. For this, the topsoil of six inches was removed and the strata of clay beneath provided material for a brick factory, which is no longer in operation.[4]

Vegetation

There was timber to be found by the streams and in groves bordering the lakes. But beyond this, there was nothing stopping the plow from being put to use as soon as the settler arrived in the spring or summer.[5]

25

Winchell and Upham found the following trees in Swift County: basswood, white or soft maple, box elder, wild plum, green ash, white elm, red or slippery elm, hackberry, burr oak, ironwood, cottonwood, prickly ash, smooth sumac, frost grape, Virginia creeper, climbing bittersweet, chokecherry, red and black raspberries, black currant, red osier dogwood, wolfberry, elder, sweet viburnum, sheepberry, and willow.[6]

Climate and Growing Season

West-central Minnesota has a transitional climate between that of the great inland valley and the continental climate of the great plains. Winters are long and severe.

The Minnesota territory, straddling the great forest region and the prairie, has a growing season of 90 to 120 frost-free days per year. Its rainfall varies between twenty and forty inches per year.*

THE INDIAN EPOCH

The earliest historical knowledge available of the territory of which Benson is an immediate part is found in the ac-

---

* Natural factors, such as these, do exert an impact upon the kind of social life and community formation which may emerge. Corn, wheat, dairying were identified, from the first, with regions of tall grasslands. Anything below 20 inches of rain per year means irrigation. Minnesota, averaging 27 inches of rain per year, did not have irrigation problems typically.

26

counts of two Jesuit missionaries, Charles Raymbault and Isaac Jacques, discoverers of Lake Superior, who, in 1641, were told of a mighty river to the westward, the Mississippi, on which dwelt the nation of the Naduesioux, the Dakota, or the Sioux.[7]

In his *History of Minnesota,* Folwell notes that two Frenchmen, Groseilliers and Radisson, were the first white men to set foot on Minnesota land, coming into contact with the Sioux about 1660 at Knife Lake in Kanabec County. France laid claim to all the land from the head of the Mississippi River to Arkansas, and from Lake Michigan to the Rocky Mountains. The part known as the Northeast Sector (including Minnesota) was held by the Dakota, the most powerful of the tribes of the Sioux Nation. Groseilliers and Radisson referred to these as the "nation of the beefe" due to their expertise in all matters having to do with buffalo. According to early Minnesota Executive Documents, Father Jacques Marquette, Father Hennepin, and numerous *coureurs de bois* conducted the first expeditions into this sector of the Minnesota territory.[8]

In 1862 LaSalle laid claim to the whole of the Father River (Mississippi) Valley in the name of Louis the Great of France, by legal rights of discovery and expedition.[9] On May 8, 1689, Nicholas Perrot, commissioner commandant of the Westward Territories, named by the governor-general of Canada, Marquis de Denonville, laid claim in the king's name to the counties and waterways inhabited by the Naduesioux (Sioux).[10] The land itself and its few rugged inhabitants were hardly affected by technical questions of claim and anticlaim.[11] During this phase, 1689–1764, French

27

fur traders and missionaries roamed the region, but no real attempt was made to set up permanent communities.[12]

France was forced to relinquish her claims to all important territories in America by the British. And to foil Great Britain, France—in the secret treaty of November 3, 1762—legally delivered to Spain all the territory west of the Mississippi.[13] Henry Adams in his *History of the United States* and Paxson in his *History of the American Frontier* both point out another secret treaty, San Ildefonso, of October 1, 1800, whereby Napoleon succeeded in regaining this land, technically, for France.[14] The land on which Benson was to be built was not finally established as an integral part of the United States until action was taken on March 10, 1804.[15]

Ambitious to rebuild a great colonial empire, Napoleon succeeded in regaining the territory by secret treaty. But with the destruction of his colonial army in Santo Domingo, and the prospect of a last-ditch fight with England, Bonaparte's designs were shattered. The United States vigorously protested changes in ownership, once word of the secret treaty became known in 1801 and when Spain announced the closing of the Mississippi in 1802. The United States offered to purchase New Orleans and the two Floridas for $2 million, and Napoleon astonished everyone with an offer to sell all of Louisiana. On April 30, 1803, the United States agreed to pay $11,250,000 for the territory and to assume $3,750,000 of French liabilities to American citizens. Formal delivery of the upper province was made to the American government at Saint Louis on March 10, 1804.

The stage was set by this last legal-political interchange between the United States and France for the potential settlement of Benson in the continental United States.[16]

West-central Minnesota territory, however, was unstable for all ordinary purposes. The pragmatic law of the frontier obtained. As late as March or April, 1838, a massacre occurred.

In early spring of 1838, a party of Sioux hunters with women and children started up the Chippewa River on their annual spring hunt. With the party was Gideon Pond, a missionary who was also something of an early anthropologist. The first night out, the hunters did not erect tents, but slept in blankets on the banks of the river, hungry because they had not yet found game. Reaching Chippewa Forks the next day, they encountered spring floods. So Tatemima ("Round Wind"), who had been camped on the far side of the forks for several weeks, spent two days ferrying the hunters, wives, and children over the high waters to his camp. That night, Tatemima's tent, twelve feet in diameter, held fifteen persons, a number of dogs, tools and baggage, and numerous children. For a week or two, the hunters left and roamed northward up the Chippewa and into upland lakes on a food-gathering expedition. Three lodges had been left behind at Tatemima's encampment to house the women and children while the hunters were away. One evening, the women and children were approached by a group of nine Chippewa Indians, led by Hole-in-the-Day, the Gull River Chippewa chief. Hole-in-the-Day communicated peaceful intentions to the women and children encamped in Tatemima's tent. The Sioux women took in the Chippewas and fed them roast dog meat and put them up in the encampment for the evening. But after the Sioux women and children had fallen asleep, the Chippewas arose and systematically murdered young and old alike except for one young Sioux woman who was taken away with them. However, one older Sioux woman and one small Sioux boy—both severely wounded—had found hiding places amid some bushes during the massacre and went unnoticed until the Chippewas had left the scene. The woman made a litter for the wounded boy and for her scalped, dead infant by fastening two poles to a horse that had been left behind and began her search for the Sioux hunting party north along the river. She succeeded in locating her men, who returned, grief-stricken, to the site—near the present locus of Benson—where the dead were still scattered. With a hoe and clamshell devices, they dug a common grave for their murdered people, and buried the mutilated bodies of seven persons. They obtained revenge two years later, in 1840, at the bloody battle of Rum River where seventy Chippewas paid with their lives for the deed of 1838.[17]

Throughout the Benson area, arrowheads and tools have been found and identified as cultural artifacts of these tribes. Some families in Benson have collections of artifacts, which they have found over the years on their property.*

The situation found by the first permanent white settlers was as follows:

* For example, on the former Edward A. Pederson farm, just outside Benson on the shores of Lake Hassel, a large number of Indian artifacts have been found and have been maintained by the family in a collection for historical purposes.

SMALL TOWN AND THE NATION

. . . the first white men found that the Indian had long been an occupant of Minnesota. Villages, widely scattered, located on lake or river, had been established. Largely because of the continual warfare with the eastern tribes, these villages were bigger than usual and better protected. The cabins were covered with well-dried deer skin, carefully stitched to keep out the cold. Tobacco alone was cultivated. Marquette found that the aborigines did not know the art of seeding before the coming of the white man. In the late summer the villagers turned out to harvest a wild marsh rice, or rye, which grew abundantly in the nearby lakes and sloughs. It was nutritive, and enough was known about its preparation to make it a tasty food. Game was the chief source of food and clothing, the latter of which was entirely of skins. The natives were warlike, savage barbarians, of the Stone Age. In the use of the bow and arrow, the warriors and hunters were very skillful. Marquette relates that the dexterity was so great that "in a moment they (arrows) fill the air." "In the Parthian mode they turn their heads in flight, and discharge their arrows so rapidly that they are no less to be feared in their retreat than in their attack."[18]

Geologic surveys reveal prehistoric Indian settlements were present on and near the current site of Benson, Minnesota.[19] For half a century into the period of white settlement, the Benson area was a bloody "no-man's-land" between the Chippewa and the Sioux.

In the early eighteenth century, the Chippewa, who were of Algonquin stock, had pushed westward out of Wisconsin and into what is now Minnesota. The Sioux, not ready to see outsiders come in and dominate their land, fought fiercely to retain their old hunting rights and villages. The Sioux were finally driven westward and southward and

31

were pinched into crowded quarters west of the Mississippi River and south of the Crow Wing River. The defeated Sioux took the Minnesota River region as their sector. What was later Benson, Minnesota, was part of the fringe area between these two warring Indian peoples. After 1804, when the United States took over this territory, government agents tried to make peace between the two warring tribes. At Prairie du Chien, August 19, 1826, a treaty set a boundary line between the two tribes' domains such that the site of Benson was definitely within the realm of the Sioux. But the treaty did not mean perfect boundaries, and violence continued for roughly fifty years into the century.[20]

Additional groupings of Indians were also present even though their roles were not as significant as the Chippewas and the Sioux.

Sisitonwans, thought to mean Marsh Villagers, and, Wahpetonwans, Villagers of the Leaves, were driven southward to the Minnesota River and undoubtedly hunted game in what was to be the future site of Benson. In 1834, it is known that these two groups had villages in several locations around western Minnesota, although neither established permanent villages in Benson's site. All in all, these lesser tribes did not number more than 4,000. Such a population may seem small, but considering their dependence on the chase for food, many more would have meant starvation.[21]

SMALL TOWN AND THE NATION

1. Stanley Holte Anonsen, *A History of Swift County* (Benson, Minn.: Swift County Historical Society, 1929), p. 1.

2. *Ibid.,* pp. 1–2.

3. *Ibid.,* p. 2.

4. *Ibid.,* p. 2.

5. *Ibid.,* p. 2.

6. N. H. Winchell and Warren Upham, *The Geology of Minnesota* (Saint Paul: St. Paul Pioneer Press Co., 1889), vol. 2, chap. 39, p. 210.

7. William Watts Folwell, *History of Minnesota* (Saint Paul: Minnesota Historical Society, 1921–1930), 1:6.

8. *Ibid.,* pp. 10, 79–80.

9. *Minnesota Executive Documents, 1876* (Saint Paul: Minnesota Historical Society, 1876), 1:945–960.

10. Folwell, *History of Minnesota,* pp. 36–38.

11. Anonsen, *A History of Swift County,* p. 4.

12. *Ibid.,* p. 4.

13. Folwell, *History of Minnesota,* p. 52.

14. *Ibid.,* pp. 79–80. *See also* Henry Adams, *History of the United States* (New York: Scribners, 1889–1891), 1:22–100; or F. L. Paxon, *History of the American Frontier* (Boston: Houghton Mifflin, 1924), pp. 130–139.

15. Anonsen, *A History of Swift County,* p. 4.

16. *Ibid.,* p. 4.

17.   N. H. Winchell, *The Aborigines of Minnesota* (Saint Paul: St. Paul Pioneer Press Co., 1911), pt. 8, chap. 1, pp. 381–383, 399–408.

18.   Anonsen, *A History of Swift County,* p. 4.

19.   Winchell, *The Aborigines of Minnesota,* pp. 201–203. Winchell describes some of these mounds, upon which the hypothesis is based, as follows:

(a) NW ¼, NW ¼, Section 5, T. 121, R. 42; (Moyer township) about 80 feet above the bottomland, on cultivated land. Group contains six tumuli, the largest two being Nos. 3 and 4, which are, respectively, 60 feet in diameter. Nos. 1 and 2 have been excavated. Surveyed May 8, 1894.

(b) SE ¼, SE ¼, Section 31, T. 122, R. 42; about 70 feet above bottomland; two tumuli, each 65 feet in diameter; one 3½ feet and the other 3 feet in height. Mr. George Wright has reported a single mound a few rods northwest of the ¼ Section corner between Sections 14 and 15, T. 122, R. 39 (Benson township) 10 feet high.

20.   Anonsen, *A History of Swift County,* p. 6.

21.   *Ibid.,* p. 7.

SMALL TOWN AND THE NATION

3

HISTORICAL
SKETCH

The Europeans who first came to the Benson area as fur traders, missionaries, and government agents wrought changes in the lives of the Indians. In Anonsen's summary:

It was natural that contact with civilization should produce changes in the lives of these savages. Some proved beneficial; others were distinctly harmful. Iron replaced the earthware and wooden utensils; the gun became the chief weapon, and cloth took the place of skins and furs in much of the clothing. The commercializing of the hunt by the great fur companies soon diminished the supply of game, making it impossible to remain long in villages as of old. Intoxicating liquors brought degeneration, while the Christian missionaries found the conversion of the natives not an easy task. They chose to cling to their old beliefs in many gods, convinced that in all objects, animate and inanimate, lived a spirit. Though the Dakotas were supposedly polygamists, it was not very common to see a man with more than one wife; whom he secured by purchase not by courtship. It is a common opinion that the men were shiftless and lazy, but as long as the family had to be supported by the products of the hunt, the labor was undoubtedly quite equally divided, the women doing the hard labor about the camp. It was only by the most strenuous efforts that the husband kept his family from starving, or being killed off by hostile tribes. When the government started the custom of annuities, however, and the game had vanished, the proverbial indolence of the Indian developed very rapidly. During this later period a little corn was planted, for the white man had taught the Aborigines how to seed. It was cultivated and harvested by the women whose only implement was the hoe. Samuel Pond estimated that only enough corn was raised to feed the whole population for two weeks at the most.[1]

Like the Indians, the early settlers were living on a bare subsistence level, much of the time about two weeks away from starvation. Much of the individual's energies were absorbed in surviving from day to day. This mentality of its pioneering days persists even to the present in the worldview of many Bensonites.

Self-sufficiency is highly prized. There is much con-

SMALL TOWN AND THE NATION

cern for the decreasing autonomy of Benson and the dependence of individuals on remote institutions over which there is a lack of local control.

THE INDIAN PERIOD

Samuel Pond, who estimated that the early settlers were rarely more than two weeks away from starvation, also kept careful notes on the dietary habits of the Indians:

> . . . for the first evening meal at Round Wind's tent, Little Crow (later famous for his leading role in the Massacre of 1862) and his wife brought in a half bushel of young turtles. Others brought an otter, a crane, and two or three ducks. The turtles were cooked alive and served in the same water in which they had been scalded to death. . . . the hostess carefully also served decayed fish to appease hunger when food was short.[2]

The summers meant greater ease in food-gathering, with an abundance of wild foods available: berries, plums, nuts, and wild vegetables. Anonsen writes about these food sources of the summer months:

> . . . the more common were the psinchincha, a root about half as large as a hen's egg, the mdo, the psincha, the wild turnip (The Pomme de Terre got its name from the abundance of these turnips growing along its banks.), the water lily, and also, wild rice. It would usually take a day of hard labor to collect a peck of roots. Deer, ducks,

geese, a few elk, bears, and buffalo furnished the meat. Dogs, horses, and muskrats were also eaten, the first named being considered a delicacy. The streams furnished fish and turtles.[3]

Trading posts and missionary establishments played virtually no role in the settlement of Swift County. The missionaries roamed rather than settled. The nearest trading post was that at Lac Qui Parle, where Joseph Renville was stationed. Another was at Lake Traverse, under Hazen Moores. The single mission in the area was established by the Reverend Thomas S. Williamson at Lac Qui Parle in July of 1835.[4]

Between 1805 and 1862 the Indians were pressed from their territory by the white settlers. The Sioux massacre of 1862 was their last stand. While the United States was technically sovereign in the American territories that she had secured from foreign governments, a long series of conferences and power-confrontations brought about ultimate Indian cessions, in 1858 and, finally, in 1862. Even in 1861, in Monson Lake, near the site of Benson, a group of thirteen were murdered by Indians.[5] By 1862, the Indian Wars in Minnesota were over.

POST–CIVIL WAR SETTLEMENTS

Waves of immigrants surged into the West in the post–Civil War period. The Homestead Act of 1862, which gave

SMALL TOWN AND THE NATION

land free to those who settled and developed it, was a strong incentive. The Scandinavians and Germans, who constituted the majority of immigrants into Swift County and the Benson area, were primarily peasant farmers, artisans, and small businessmen.

Typically, an individual or two from a family came first, to be joined after an interval by other family members. Families constituted the major units of migration and community formation. After the great Sioux Indian uprising of 1862 the territory became, unequivocally, safe for settlement.

The first white settler in the Benson area is thought to be Ole Corneliusen, a Norwegian, who arrived on foot from Olmstead County in 1866. Foot travel was the normal means by which early settlers in the area visited Saint Cloud, Minnesota, from Benson for supplies, a trip that took from several weeks to a month.

The next settler, after the arrival of Ole Corneliusen, was Lars Christenson, also Norwegian, who came by ox team from Wisconsin in charge of a party of settlers. The party divided into two groups, settling on the Chippewa River and nearby Camp Lake, respectively. The railroad was soon thereafter extended from Minneapolis to nearby Delano, providing easy access to the Minneapolis area.

The railroad became a major factor in further developments. By 1869, the Saint Paul and Pacific Railroad had reached Willmar, a mere thirty miles from Benson. The Saint Paul and Pacific Railroad was integrated into the Great Northern in 1885, linking Kerkhoven, DeGraff, Benson, and Clontarf like beads on a single transportation

39
———
Historical Sketch

chain. The depot center, set early in Benson, established contact with Minneapolis, Chicago and points east and west.

COMMUNITY GROWTH

Benson's first general store was erected in 1869 by A. W. and W. V. Lathrop. A second competitive general store, of sod, was built in 1869.

The year 1869 was a lively one for Benson. For more than a year, Benson was the westward terminus of the Great Northern railroad tracks. As an outpost of civilization for this brief period, Benson was the contact point for the famous Red River Carts, whose cargoes were loaded onto the trains for shipment into Minneapolis–Saint Paul.

The carts were built of wood and rawhide and were pulled by oxen. They traveled in trains, and the scream of their wheels could be heard for miles. They carried goods from Benson to Fort Abercrombie, which was located some fifteen miles downstream from the site of present-day Wahpeton, from whence goods were carted as far as Fort Garry (Winnipeg).

At this time, Benson served as a market center for a territory a hundred miles westward, northward, and southward, being the point where the railroad from the East met the ox cart from unsettled lands. Wheat was hauled from Lac Qui Parle, Chippewa, Big Stone, Stevens, Pope, Douglas, and Yellow Medicine counties, and goods for field and house were purchased in Benson for the return trips.

Prices were high for the times: a barrel of pork cost $40; 100 pounds of flour, $5; very poor butter, $1 per pound. Eggs were a luxury; potatoes were scarce.

In February of 1870, by an enabling act of the Minnesota state legislature, the twenty-one most northern townships in Chippewa County were removed to form Swift County as a separate administrative unit. Benson was named by railroad tycoons after a prominent politician from Anoka. The naming of Swift County is obscure, possibly after a Minnesota governor or a state representative from Chippewa County. The first county board met in the Lathrop store in January of 1871. Benson's city government became operational in April of the same year.

By 1876, the population of Benson had grown to 300; there were four general stores, two drugstores, two machinery houses, three hotels, one bank, and two saloons. In one of the general stores, A. N. Johnson and Co., the sales soared to $60,000 in the last eight months of 1875. During this eight-month period of 1875 in Benson, sales comprised 1.5 million feet of lumber, 1,260,000 shingles, 170,000 laths, 380 reapers, 380 mowers, 380 harvesters, 240 seeders, 10 thrashing machine rigs, 160 plows, 137 wagons, and 61 sulky hayracks.

The first hotel, the Emigrant House, was constructed by the railroad company to handle railway workers, migrants, and travelers. In 1876, an addition was built to the hotel, which was renamed the Pacific House. In 1900, the structure was moved to a lot behind the light plant and renamed the Columbia Hotel. On the previous site of the Pacific House was erected a new brick hotel with forty-five rooms, the Paris Hotel.

The first school classes were held in the Emigrant House Hotel in 1870, with Mrs. Charlotte Knowlton as teacher. In 1871, Benson's first school was built. The first graduate was to receive a high-school diploma from Benson public schools in 1890. In 1904, the northside school was constructed; in 1913, the southside school. The southside school was used for lower grades; the northside for high school.

TABLE 2

POPULATION OF BENSON:
SELECTED INTERVALS; U.S. CENSUS

YEAR	Population Total
1876	300
1880	457
1890	877
1900	1,525
1910	1,677
1920	2,111
1930	2,095
1940	2,729
1950	3,398
1960	3,678

Source: *U.S. Census Reports* (Washington, D.C.: U.S. Government Printing Office, 1880–1960); Benson, in Swift County, Minnesota.

SMALL TOWN AND THE NATION

The population grew from 300 people in 1876 to nearly 4,000 at present.

A moderate population growth, with exception of the period 1920–1930, occurred. In the 1920s and 1930s, the Depression years when Lake Hassel near Benson was dry, over half the families in Swift County were at one time or another on the welfare rolls.

Among special crises that left their mark on the community were the smallpox epidemic of 1872, the grasshopper plague of 1876, and the fire of 1880. The fire, Benson's counterpart of many similar urban catastrophes of the time, was started by a cigar butt dropped into a knothole in the floor at Joe Foutain's Saloon. The cigar ignited a fire that destroyed a whole city block, dealing severe losses to twenty business places. As a result of its "Armageddon," Benson organized its first volunteer fire department on June 18, 1881.

Benson constructed a waterworks in 1895 and served as a model of efficient community action for other nearby villages. In 1894, 4,000 feet of sewage lines were laid for community use. In 1901, the construction of cement sidewalks was begun. In 1893, Benson acquired its first telephone, which operated between the office and home of Dr. C. L. Scofield three years before the original Bell patent expired. In 1904, after ten years as a local exchange system, the Benson telephone company incorporated itself into a countywide system with headquarters in Benson. A power and light plant was built by private investors just before the beginning of this century and, a few years later, in 1902, was purchased by the city of Benson as a public utility. A public library was established in Benson in 1911 through a $7,500 donation from Andrew Carnegie and supplemented by local donations by Bensonites.

In 1912, the Swift County Hospital, with a capacity of twenty to twenty-five patients, was constructed in Benson at a cost of $15,000. In 1949, sparked by the leadership of Mrs. Russell Hanson as president of the local hospital auxiliary, a new hospital was constructed. Mrs. Hanson led a group of volunteers who raised over $60,000 to help build the new hospital with the slogan, "Dig Deeper, This Time It's For Ourselves." The notable success of this local project made news around the state as a model of effective community action. From Dr. Scofield to his present-day successor, Benson has been fortunate to have at least one medical doctor throughout its history.

In 1900, Benson's first horseless carriage made its appearance. J. B. A. Benoit, who had been in the bicycle-repair business, was fascinated by the invention. He purchased a lathe in 1901 and began to build his own automobile, finishing it in April of 1902. This two-seated car had a five-horsepower Dyke engine and attained speeds of twenty miles per hour. Its first run from Benson to Clontarf, a distance of six miles, took twenty-eight minutes.

Today the county is thickly dotted with thriving groves of trees. The railroad began planting trees in 1873 as part of a program to promote the sale of railroad lands west of Kandiyohi County. Prizes were offered by individuals and newspapers to the farmer planting the most trees during each year. Beginning in 1876, the state legislature, by an

44

enabling act, appropriated sums of $20,000 to $25,000 for tree bounties.

In 1888, the law provided a payment of $2.50 an acre for six years for the planting of forests and groves. The amount expended by the state from 1876 to 1911 amounted to $600,000. The farmers of Swift County, one of the first groups to see the need of positive governmental action, were recipients of this aid each year, and as late as 1898, planted a total of 213 acres in trees, for which they received $511.50. Since the farmer appreciated the value of windbreaks, wood for fuel, fence posts, and construction, a great deal of tree planting was also done without state aid.[6]

POLITICAL ORGANIZATIONS

Benson and Swift County were areas of dominant Republicanism almost from the first records available, in 1872, up to the Great Depression of the 1930s. At this time a major shift occurred in the Farmer-Labor and Democratic-Farmer-Labor orientation.

Benson has had a history of the politics of reform-progressivism, beginning with a local Benson clergyman, O. J. Kvale, who ran as a rebel-progressive and won election to the United States Congress in the old Seventh Congressional District, which he represented until the time of his tragic death in a fire in his lake cabin. His son, Paul Kvale, then served in that office for several terms. Benson was known as a seat of Kvale progressivism.

The shift from Republicanism of the early settlement days to the Progressivism of the Great Depression period was epitomized in the person of Lewis Herfindahl, a Norwegian farmer, who was elected from Benson to serve as state representative for Swift County in the Minnesota state legislature in 1924. Herfindahl was an early supporter of Floyd Bjornsterne Olson in his drive for the governorship and became a close political associate of Governor Olson and in 1936 chairman of the Minnesota State Farmer-Labor party. This Bensonite, Lewis Herfindahl, wrote unblushingly of the masses in his tribute to Governor Floyd B. Olson, at the time of Olson's death in 1936:

> To my mind, the State of Minnesota has, through the death of Governor Olson, suffered a loss which will be felt for years. As Governor, Floyd B. Olson represented the highest type of sincerity in office. He truly represented the people. His spirit will live on, forever guiding persons of Liberal beliefs to *accomplishments for the masses.*[7]

NOTES

1. Stanley Holte Anonsen, *A History of Swift County* (Benson, Minn.: Swift County Historical Society, 1929), p. 8.

2. S. W. Pond, *Two Volunteers Among the Dakotas* (Boston: Congregationalist Sunday School Publishing Society, 1893), p. 97.

3. Anonsen, *A History of Swift County*, p. 8.

4. *Ibid.*, p. 8.

5. *Ibid.*, p. 11.

6. *Ibid.*, p. 3.

7. Lewis Herfindahl, "Tribute No. 26," in *Floyd B. Olson: Minnesota's Greatest Liberal Governor, A Memorial Volume*, eds. John S. McGrath and James J. Delmont (Saint Paul: McGrath and Delmont, 1937), p. 163.

4

SOCIAL
STRUCTURE
OF
BENSON

B enson typifies the communities that just a few generations ago made up the fabric of America. Even as
recent a President as Warren Harding could speak of hap-
piness as residing in the American town. Great urban-
industrial concentrations were gaining in the late nineteeth
and early twentieth centuries, but they were experienced as
alien, foreign, un-American. The muckrakers reveled in the
exposure of *The Shame of the Cities.*

But the point of gravity of American life was shifting to the urban concentrations. A nation was forming with half its population compressed in a continuous complex of cities along the eastern seaboard: Washington, D.C., New York City, Baltimore, Philadelphia, Boston, New Haven, Augusta. Benson is a tiny community of a mere 4,000 inhabitants, in a state with more than half of its 3 million population concentrated in one metropolitan complex.

COUNTY GOVERNMENT

Politically, Benson is the central administrative unit of Swift County. The county commissioners elected in sectors across the county meet in Benson to act on county welfare, county roads, and various other county business. In autumn, a district court session convenes under the district judge, who comes from outside Benson and serves other counties of the judicial district. He is elected by voters in the many counties of his judicial district. Juvenile courts are specially designated courts in urban areas, such as Minneapolis–Saint Paul, but in Benson, the probate judge, elected in Swift County to preside over probate matters, also handles juvenile cases. In the courthouse, there are also offices for the following departments of county administration: county welfare, veterans' service officer, county treasurer, supervisor of assessments, superintendent of county schools (over those

49

rural schools still in operation), county sheriff, register of deeds, county nurse, judge of probate, county health officer, extension service, county engineer, county coroner, clerk of court, auditor, and county attorney.

MUNICIPAL GOVERNMENT

Benson maintains a municipal government that operates from a municipal building built with federal assistance during the New Deal era. City offices include: city attorney, city clerk, city disposal plant, city fire hall and volunteer city fire department, city light plant, municipal liquor store, Benson public library, street maintenance, water and light maintenance, and police. Benson elects a mayor and council who, together with a paid city manager, govern Benson. For much of its history the city council and mayoralty were unpaid honorific offices.

LEGAL INSTITUTIONS

Benson has nine practicing lawyers, including one who is currently register of deeds, one who is county attorney, and one who is city attorney. There are two law firms with three members each, and one firm composed of two lawyers. The firm with two lawyers includes one lawyer who resides in nearby Appleton, also in Swift County.

MEDICAL INSTITUTIONS

For its size, Benson has a large number of physicians. Five full-time resident doctors of medicine practice in Benson. One is a solo practitioner. There are two group practices with two members each.

The new hospital, built in 1949, has forty beds and is accredited by the American College of Surgeons and the American Hospital Association. The hospital was a major reason for the concentration of doctors in the city, giving Benson five of the seven practicing M.D.'s in the county (the other two practicing in nearby Appleton). In addition, Benson has an osteopathic physician who recently located in town. There are three chiropractic physicians and three optometrists in Benson.

The hospital is a city-county institution financed by taxation (two-thirds of the budget is paid for by city taxes and one third by county). The trustees of the hospital commission are named by county commissioners and the Benson city council, with specified proportions of trustees coming from county commissioner districts and the city. Surgeons come in on specified days from Willmar and Minneapolis–Saint Paul and practice specialized surgery in the hospital. The local general practitioners perform general surgery. A pathologist, from nearby Litchfield, Minnesota, maintains a pathology lab in the Benson hospital, and makes regular visits.

In addition, associate membership on the Benson hospital medical staff includes specialists from Minneapolis and Saint Paul. About ten specialists have associate staff memberships on this basis, including three radiologists from nearby Willmar.

There are two mortuaries in Benson, both operated by local residents. This is one of the few areas of Benson's life where the conflict of local and translocal forces does not occur.

RELIGIOUS INSTITUTIONS

There are nine church buildings in Benson: Our Redeemer's Lutheran, Trinity Lutheran, Saint Mark's Lutheran, Saint Francis Catholic, Christ Episcopal, Pilgrim Congregational, Assembly of God, First Baptist, and First Evangelical Free. Benson also has smaller churches in its nearby outskirts that are served on a group basis.

A Lutheran church has the largest membership, and Lutheranism exerts a dominance in the church life of Benson, though the other churches are important qualitatively in the life of the community.

52

EDUCATIONAL INSTITUTIONS

There were over one hundred sixty members in the last graduating class of the Benson High School. The school, moreover, plays an important role in the yearly social cycle. When school is out in summer there is a noticeable void in the social life of the town. With one of the largest single budgets and payrolls in the community, the board—elected in popular election—hires a school administrator to hire teachers.

The Saint Francis Catholic Church operates a parochial school. Though its enrollment is small and select, it exerts significant influence. Several Sisters are skilled musicians who take in youngsters for private lessons in a wide variety of musical pursuits. The recital of the Saint Francis music pupils is a major cultural event on the calendar each year.

Employing nearly one hundred persons as teachers alone, the Benson public schools exert a major shaping influence on the life of the community. In the fall, on Friday nights, when stores are open for shopping in town, the school plays its home football games to large audiences on the lighted athletic field named in honor of L. H. Brockmeyer, whose teams put Benson on the football map. Music department concerts and class plays attract large audiences. Basketball games are held in the winter in the West Central Conference with Glenwood, Willmar, Sauk Centre, Montevideo, Morris, and Litchfield. Benson competes favorably in all sports with these schools. Even those who have no children or who are older follow the school events.

Benson has access to higher education facilities. The new University of Minnesota at Morris four-year liberal arts college is just twenty-seven miles from Benson, and many Bensonites drive forth and back daily. The Willmar State Junior College, thirty miles to the east, also attracts Benson students.

COMMUNICATIONS

Formal institutions for communications in Benson include KBMO Radio, a 500-watt, home-owned, commercial radio station, on the air every day of the year from sunrise to sunset at 1290 kc. Local merchants advertise on its airways.

Nearby (fifty miles away) Alexandria, Minnesota, has a network-affiliate television channel that beams a first-magnitude signal into Benson. Nearly all housing units in Benson have TV sets. A portable TV set can pick up the Alexandria channel. Some Benson firms advertise on this TV station, which covers important news breaks in Benson.

Benson has had a hometown newspaper continually since the 1870s. It was originally called the Benson *Times*. On July 1, 1886, the *Monitor* was established. The paper has not missed an issue in more than 4,000 weeks, spanning eight decades. At present, there are two issues per week; the Tuesday edition is called the *News*.

In addition, the west-central Minnesota *Tribune,* published in nearby Willmar on a daily basis, has a large circulation throughout the Benson area. And there are radio stations other than Benson's in small towns in the vicinity: KWLM Willmar, KDMA Montevideo, KMRS Morris, KXRA Alexandria, KLFD Litchfield. Beaming into Benson from the Twin Cities are WCCO Radio and KSTP Radio. One familiar pattern is to listen to the Benson station for local news and to supplement this with selective listening to WCCO.

FINANCIAL INSTITUTIONS

There are two banks in Benson. One, the larger, is independent and home-owned. The other bank is a member of a chain that has its head offices outside Benson in a corporation far-removed from west-central Minnesota. Both banks are prosperous.

OTHER COMMERCIAL INSTITUTIONS

Up and down Main Street, there are businesses and merchants—both independent and affiliated with larger groupings.

On the outskirts of Benson are two relatively new firms, both of which exert an important economic influence on the town. One is Wiman, Inc., a factory that is part of a large corporation with plants all around the Midwest. It hires local labor—mostly women—to run the assembly line. The other, Tyler, Inc., with ownership located in Chicago as well as Benson, also employs Bensonites. These firms represent the new industries, as contrasted to the older, more traditional local concerns.

The Great Northern Railway tracks split Benson in two. A park with green benches stretches on either side. It is still recalled how once a train carrying Theodore Roosevelt stopped here while TR addressed Bensonites gathered around him at the tracks. On the two main streets running parallel to the tracks are located the business places: cafés, hardware stores, department stores, professional offices, and others. There are approximately four blocks of businesses on each side.

NATIONAL INSTITUTIONS

There are a growing number of federal branch offices in Benson, many having to do with conservation, soil, and wildlife. They include the following federal offices: U.S. Government Department of Agriculture Stabilization of Conservation Commission, the U.S. Fish and Wildlife Service, the Soil Conservation Office, the Post Office, the Federal Crop Insurance, the Farmers' Home Administration, and a new federal housing project that looms high in contrast to the prairie-level elevation of Benson's old structures. This new structure provides low-cost housing for older people.

Roosevelt Park stands as a sleepy small-town square-block separating the two faces of Benson. The old Victorian-appearing county courthouse faces east across its green, and facing west is the streamlined Park View Manor skyscraper.

STRUCTURAL CONFRONTATIONS

Historically, Benson demonstrated to a high degree the small-town virtues once thought to be so distinctive of America: spirited individual free enterprise, civic conscious-ness, and pride in local self-sufficiency. The large number of Benson's original institutions were locally founded and oriented inwardly to the community's needs. However, the inventory of Benson's institutional order in the mid-1960s reveals a structural confrontation of institutions locally founded, owned, and operated on the one hand and branch offices, representatives, or affiliates of translocal structures on the other.

The new hospital was formed as a product of the old type of local civic enterprise, but it was helped by federal assistance. And its authority in considerable measure derives

57

from its accreditation by the American College of Surgeons and the American Hospital Association. Moreover, its services are enhanced by associate memberships of specialists from outside Benson's city limits.

Benson's educational institutions are local, as is true everywhere else in America, but her educational needs are complemented by nearby institutions of higher learning such as the Morris branch of the University of Minnesota and the Willmar State Junior College. Thus education, too, demonstrates the confrontation of local and translocal forces.

Benson has her own communications in the form of a biweekly newspaper and locally owned radio station. But her communications are routinely complemented by various translocal news media. In Alexandria's network TV affiliate and a west-central Minnesota daily newspaper again a translocal confrontation with local forces occurs.

Of the two banks in Benson one is locally owned and independent; the other a branch bank of a distant corporation. In contrast to home-owned and home-operated industries are two relatively new firms owned and directed by outside interests. There is also a confrontation of home-owned and chain retail establishments.

Finally there are a number of branch offices of federal agencies operating on the local scene. These are in charge of a variety of services and situations that have slipped permanently from local control to be consolidated in the hands of the agencies of the federal government.

5

BENSON'S LOCALS AND COSMOPOLITANS

The historical sketch of Benson reveals it to be a product of individual enterprise, civic conscientiousness, and the desire for local self-sufficiency. However, as the mass society dominated by vast cosmopolitan and industrial complexes took shape, the relation of the small local community to the surrounding world changed. And even when the small community survived, its life was transformed by local representatives of the mass world. The contemporary social structure of Benson was seen to present a confrontation of institutions from the old local and the translocal worlds.

It was anticipated that the persons whose life chances were anchored in these two institutional complexes tend to develop distinct life-styles and pursue different strategies. The one group, locals, would tend to press the community in the direction of self-sufficiency; the other group, cosmopolitans, would tend to orient life to the centers of outside power. To some extent, both forces could be expected to operate on everyone, but to a different degree.

Because Benson on its own cannot assimilate all of its own children, Bensonites face the prospect that some of their offspring must make their way in the wider world. Benson's parents must either prepare their offspring for the metropolitan world or decrease their own children's chances for success outside Benson. However, this very preparation for life outside may itself encourage the children to leave. In their view of education, Bensonites could be expected to be ambivalent. The whole sphere of socialization is subject to conflicting pulls.

Benson's economy, too, is caught in a crossfire of localism and translocalism. Economic power increasingly resides outside Benson. In the colloquial speech of one old-time Bensonite: "Nowadays, all the marbles are held by other hands; it's no longer like when I was a boy and President Teddy Roosevelt's train pulled up for a full stop in Benson and TR himself got out and talked to those who had driven their buggies up near the tracks. . . . Can you imagine a U.S. President stopping in Benson today? Population was strung out in those days, and we had some of the marbles in small towns. No more."

Economically, Benson is a service center to farmers in an immediate vicinity, and in this respect Benson today seems to differ little from the Benson of the past. The farmers still come to buy goods and obtain services. Local prosperity is still tied to agriculture. Drought would hit Benson hard today, as it did in the 1930s when Lake Hassel was dry as a bone and the farmers tried to salvage hay from the lake bottom. But drought today would be mitigated by aid from the federal government. There are other ways in which the local economic tie is severed. Farmers sign agreements directly with the federal government as to the use of their land for diverted acres or to put it in the Soil Bank, etc. Benson was unable by itself to provide housing of the quality that the federal government provided in Park View Manor. Nor could Benson by itself provide the massive programs for farmers today, or for employment of area young people in the Neighborhood Youth Corps, etc.

Recognizing this dualism in Benson's institutional life today, the present study sought to devise an instrument that would measure differential reactions to it by old-time entrepreneurs on Main Street on the one hand and younger Bensonites or Bensonites working for chain stores or teaching in town on the other. There are wage-earners in Benson whose income comes directly from translocal sources, in contrast to wage-earners associated with home-owned businesses. There are independent entrepreneurs and representatives of outside economic concerns. The career civil servant in a federal government branch in Benson receives his salary from the federal government in contrast to the locally paid official.

THE ANALYTIC SURVEY

A series of hypotheses were developed around the major hypothesis that Benson is internally torn by the contrasting forces of the local and national community. This major hypothesis is that two systems of community formation, the local and the national, establish the primary lines of cleavage in Benson's social life. Specific hypotheses were advanced to account for characteristics of old-style Bensonites (presumed to be oriented more toward traditional localism) as compared to the characteristics of new-style Bensonites (presumed to be oriented more toward the wider world). The specific hypotheses advanced were as follows:

I. The lines of tension between local and nonlocal forces are discernible in the economy of Benson.

II. Benson's structure of power and influence is polarized in terms of local and nonlocal interests.

III. The major lines of stress in Benson's institutions of socialization arise from the conflict of local and non-local interests.

Besides the sample of old-style Bensonites and new-style Bensonites, a sample of ex-Bensonites (persons who for some reason had left Benson) was also drawn. Thus, three-way comparisons were indicated: old-style versus new-style Bensonites, old-style versus ex-Bensonites, new-style versus ex-Bensonites. Fifty old-style Bensonites were sampled. These were persons whose occupations were local in nature: farmers operating their own small, family farms; operators of small businesses that are self-owned; employees of the home-owned independent stores; long-time Bensonites whose "free enterprises" have become "landmarks" in town; and those whose independent enterprises appeared in keeping with traditional Benson.

Fifty new-style Bensonites were sampled. These were persons whose occupations were translocal in nature: managers of translocal firms in Benson, employees whose work is for nonhome-owned enterprises, owners of "factory" farms, professionals in Benson just for a stop "on their way up" in their field, managers of stores with a branch in Benson.

Finally, fifty persons were sampled who had once resided in Benson but who had since moved elsewhere. Such ex-Bensonites were to be used chiefly as a control group for the analytical study. Persons who had left Benson were assumed to differ from the persons they left behind. The group of primary interest to the present study were the old-style and new-style Bensonites.

A questionnaire (instrument) having to do with social data and social attitudes was developed to gather data for testing the hypothesis concerning the sample groups. The hypotheses predicted a cleavage in social characteristics, attitudes, and life-styles between old- and new-style Bensonites and between both and ex-Bensonites.

The analytical instrument was in standardized written form and comprised sections on social data and social attitudes. A letter to Bensonites was provided as an introduction. The first twenty-two questions assembled basic social data such as age, schooling, religious affiliation, marital status, finances, politics and nationality of the respondent. Part II of the questionnaire was composed of a number of measurements of social attitudes. These were in the form of statements to which the respondent was asked to circle SA if he strongly agrees, A if he agrees, D if he disagrees, and SD if he strongly disagrees. There were forty-three of these opinion statements, relating to economic orientation, socialization, and social control in Benson today. Thus, hypothetically, if old-style Bensonites tended to react in a pronouncedly different way to a given opinion than did the new-style Bensonites—for example, on an attitude of socialization—then different social strategies could be expected.

ADMINISTRATION OF THE INSTRUMENT

Members of the sample were given the questionnaire, along with a self-addressed, stamped envelope—provided so that the respondents could drop the completed questionnaire into the mail. The sample of old-style and new-style Bensonites were given their questionnaires in person, but the ex-Bensonites (who were scattered from coast to coast) were sent their questionnaires along with a stamped envelope for return.

Of the total of fifty questionnaires for each subgroup in the sample, the return was as follows (after several follow-up promptings): thirty-eight old-style Bensonites, thirty-seven new-style Bensonites, and thirty-five ex-Bensonites.

SOCIAL CHARACTERISTICS
OF THE SAMPLE

Data were gathered from the sample groups on a number of social characteristics: age, education, religious affiliation, family ties, occupational roles, income levels, property claims, level of conspicuous consumption, party affiliations, organizational memberships, officerships, clique affiliations, and standing in class hierarchy. It was anticipated that the three sample groups would differ as to these various characteristics. Old-style Bensonites were anticipated to be older, less educated, more religious, more traditional in economic characteristics, and more localistic in control traits. New-style Bensonites were anticipated to be the least traditional. Ex-Bensonites were anticipated to fall between the other two samples.

TABLE 3

AGE OF RESPONDENTS

AGE	Old-Style	New-Style	Ex-Bensonites
20–30 years	1	4	5
31–40 years	3	17	9
41–50 years	10	12	9
51 years and over	24	4	12
Total	38	37	35

Both in the sample taken for the present study, and in the population studied in the field at large in Benson today, the old-style Bensonite whose loyalty is still anchored in locality is, typically, an older person. There are exceptions, such as the younger person who inherits the home-owned

TABLE 4

EDUCATION OF RESPONDENTS

HIGHEST EDUCATION COMPLETED	Old-Style	New-Style	Ex-Bensonites
Some grade school	2	0	0
Completed grade school	6	1	0
Some high school	4	4	1
Completed high school	7	10	9
Some college	11	13	11
Completed college	4	5	10
Hold graduate degrees	4	4	4
Total	38	37	35

investment of his father, but the old-style Bensonite is disappearing.

The new-style Bensonites in the sample have had more years of formal education than the old-style, and ex-Bensonites reveal a higher completion rate at college than either of the others. Youngsters growing up in Benson increasingly wish to succeed in a wider world and display an increased interest in specialized advanced education. Old-style Bensonites grew up in a time when a high school diploma was sufficient. New-style Bensonites take the high school diploma as a mere preliminary step.

Religious affiliation was claimed by all who returned questionnaires. The churches in Benson, in fact, have more people on their official membership rolls than Benson's 1960 official census population. The local newspaper gives the pastors space at Christmas to write meditations on the meaning of the season. Benson's children grow up to respect the pastors and church schoolteachers. Benson's properties as a traditional small town are manifest in its resistance to the typical erosion of the urban church.

TABLE 5

RELIGIOUS AFFILIATIONS OF RESPONDENTS

RELIGION	Old-Style	New-Style	Ex-Bensonites
Catholic	6	3	1
Protestant	32	34	34
Other	0	0	0
Total	38	37	35

Benson's Locals and Cosmopolitans

It should, of course, be noted that Americans tend to retain formal religious membership even while drifting away from the church. Hence the picture is not complete until one studies the facts of church attendance. Furthermore, in a small town or city everyone is more visible and subject to the scrutiny of neighbors. This may keep formal church membership high though, in fact, interest is waning. Moreover, in a small town it is possible for a clergyman to exercise constant vigilance in a manner not possible in an urban setting.

In Benson, which is primarily a Protestant community, it was anticipated that the Catholics would be more heavily represented among old-style than new-style types because of the generally greater traditionalism of the Catholic Church. There was a slight difference in this respect. It was also anticipated that Protestants would be more mobile and would be overrepresented among ex-Bensonites. Here, too, there was a slight difference in the predicted direction.

It was also anticipated that old-style Bensonites would more often be married than new-style or ex-Bensonites. While there was a difference in marital status between Bensonites and ex-Bensonites in the anticipated direction, none of the new-style Bensonites sampled was unmarried. It is possible that getting married may be a factor in keeping new-style Bensonites in Benson.

Of the sample subgroups, the ex-Bensonites had the largest proportion of those who said their parents were Benson-born. However, as anticipated, more old-style Bensonites were of exclusively locally derived parents.

Historically Benson is primarily a Norwegian com-

TABLE 6

MARITAL STATUS OF RESPONDENTS

STATUS	Old-Style	New-Style	Ex-Bensonites
Married	34	37	26
Unmarried	4	0	9
Total	38	37	35

TABLE 7

BIRTHPLACE OF RESPONDENTS' PARENTS

BIRTHPLACE	Old-Style	New-Style	Ex-Bensonites
Benson	9	3	11
Not Benson	29	34	24
Total	38	37	35

munity. Other Scandinavian groups and Germans form major subgroups. Old-style Bensonites—heavily weighted toward Norwegian nationality—reflect Benson's settlement by Norwegians and the early domination by them. As anticipated, the proportion of Norwegians is also high among ex-Bensonites, but among new-style Bensonites the proportion of Norwegians decreases. Still, in Benson today, Scandinavian influence is everywhere present, and while their relative number is decreasing proportionately, there are still those who pride themselves on their ability to converse in fluent Norwegian.

TABLE 8

NATIONALITY OF RESPONDENTS

NATIONALITY	Old-Style	New-Style	Ex-Bensonites
Norwegian	25	10	19
German	4	10	8
Other	9	17	8
Total	38	37	35

TABLE 9

OCCUPATIONS OF RESPONDENTS

OCCUPATION	Old-Style	New-Style	Ex-Bensonites
Farmer	3	0	5
Laborer	7	2	0
White-collar worker	2	3	1
Professional	10	15	15
Businessman	8	10	5
Other	8	7	9
Total	38	37	35

The economic characteristics of the samples were expected to differ in a number of ways. Farmers appear among old-style and ex-Bensonites, but not in the new-style group. Among the old-style Bensonites, the idea remains that the work of a man is directly related to his masculinity, and that it should be physical. It is beneath a man to be totally free of an ability to pitch in and work alongside the men in the field, said one old-style Bensonite. Many new-style Bensonites are removed by a generation from the Great Depression, and this provides the basis for an attitudinal gulf between the groups. The pathos of the Great Depression, ever fresh in the memory of those Bensonites who lived through it, finds its way into their opinions on work and economics. One older man in Benson said that things were so bleak in the 1930s in Benson that hitchhikers offered to go *either* east *or* west on Highway 12 if they could obtain a free ride.

Many old-style Bensonites are concerned that the typical new-style citizen is salaried in a Benson institution with translocal ties. The findings of the three subgroups in the sample, however, indicate quite similar tendencies in the distribution of income among the three groups. Although the ex-Bensonites showed a heavier concentration in the $10,000–$11,999 income category, there were more resident Bensonites with yearly incomes of $12,000 and over. In all three subsamples, there would appear to be a tendency either

TABLE 10

YEARLY INCOME REPORTED BY RESPONDENTS

INCOME	Old-Style	New-Style	Ex-Bensonites
Under $5,000	8	5	6
$5,000–$7,999	12	13	10
8,000– 9,999	4	8	5
10,000–11,999	7	4	10
12,000 and over	7	7	4
Total	38	37	35

TABLE 11

VALUE OF RESPONDENTS' INVESTMENTS IN TOOLS

VALUE	Old-Style	New-Style	Ex-Bensonites
Under $100	16	18	17
$100–$299	2	5	1
300– 499	3	0	2
500– 999	0	2	1
1,000 and over	17	12	14
Total	38	37	35

TABLE 12

VALUE OF RESPONDENTS' BUSINESSES OR OTHER INVESTMENTS

VALUE	Old-Style	New-Style	Ex-Bensonites
No Investment	18	20	15
Under $10,000	5	7	8
$10,000–$29,999	5	8	6
30,000– 49,999	3	1	2
50,000 and over	7	1	4
Total	38	37	35

for a very small investment (under $100) or a quite heavy investment ($1,000 and over) in tools. The same pattern appears for other investments as well. None of the new-style Bensonites was on welfare or had pension assistance. Eight of the old-style respondents indicated they were on some form of old-age assistance.

TABLE 13

EXTENT OF SOCIAL WELFARE AND PENSION ASSISTANCE AMONG RESPONDENTS

CATEGORY	Old-Style	New-Style	Ex-Bensonites
Recipients	8	0	4
Nonrecipients	30	37	31
Total	38	37	35

TABLE 14

VALUE OF RESPONDENTS' HOUSES

VALUE	Old-Style	New-Style	Ex-Bensonites
Under $10,000	10	13	14
$10,000–$14,999	11	13	10
15,000– 19,999	13	10	8
20,000– 29,999	4	1	2
30,000 and over	0	0	1
Total	38	37	35

The category of "under $10,000" is biased because some respondents checked it as an alternative since they owned no house.

Of the thirty-eight old-style Bensonites in the sample, only two rent, and thirty-six are homeowners. Of thirty-seven new-style Bensonites in the sample, twelve rent and twenty-five are homeowners. Of the thirty-five ex-Bensonites, seven rent. This would tend to follow expected patterns with the

73

TABLE 15

RENTERS AMONG RESPONDENTS

MONTHLY RENT	Old-Style	New-Style	Ex-Bensonites
Under $55	1	3	3
$55–$69	0	2	1
70– 84	1	5	1
85 and over	0	2	2
Total	2	12	7

more settled old-style residents anchored into their town in their own homes, and the more mobile new-style Bensonites tending more to rent. There is, though, in Benson's new-style citizens a strong tendency to begin payments on one's own home rather than rent—even knowing one's stay in Benson is likely to be quite temporary, for homes at present are sold easily in Benson.

The automobile is an important factor in Benson today, as its advent and increased use by all levels of Bensonites

TABLE 16

NUMBER OF CARS OWNED BY RESPONDENTS

NUMBER OF CARS	Old-Style	New-Style	Ex-Bensonites
None	4	1	4
One	21	25	19
Two or more	13	11	12
Total	38	37	35

TABLE 17

POLITICAL PREFERENCE OF RESPONDENTS

PREFERENCE	Old-Style	New-Style	Ex-Bensonites
Republican	21	25	21
Democratic	16	11	13
No Preference	1	1	1
Total	38	37	35

have torn geographical anchorage to shreds. No significant differences appear between the groups in automobile ownership.

Benson's political history has been dominated by Republicanism from settlement to the Depression in the 1930s, which brought increased awareness of the need for government assistance. Bensonites interviewed prided themselves on their independence and their preference for voting for a man and not a party. A careful scrutiny of Benson's political voting behavior over the last several decades indicates this is true. But in the end, the traditional Bensonite is most inclined toward the Republican party.

Persons in large urban centers often dream of the small town as a withdrawn quiet place with plenty of time for reflection. Yet persons in small towns typically find themselves in a bewildering whirl of local organizational life with little time to themselves. The organizational involvement typical of the small town has affected all classes of Bensonites, although, as anticipated, old-style Bensonites show greater local organizational affiliations than do the other two groups.

75

TABLE 18

NUMBER OF ORGANIZATIONS
REGULARLY ATTENDED BY RESPONDENTS

NUMBER OF ORGANIZATIONS	Old-Style	New-Style	Ex-Bensonites
One	9	6	9
Two	8	11	7
Three	9	8	6
Four	2	1	5
Five	1	5	4
Six or more	4	0	0
None	5	6	4
Total	38	37	35

TABLE 19

NUMBER OF OFFICES HELD BY RESPONDENTS

NUMBER OF OFFICES	Old-Style	New-Style	Ex-Bensonites
One	11	6	7
Two	1	3	2
Three	1	2	0
Four or more	2	2	0
None	23	24	26
Total	38	37	35

One index of power in organizational affiliations is that of offices held on the local scene. No differences appear in this respect between old- and new-style Bensonites. They both differ in anticipated ways from ex-Bensonites.

TABLE 20

NUMBER OF TRANSLOCAL OFFICES HELD BY RESPONDENTS

NUMBER OF OFFICES	Old-Style	New-Style	Ex-Bensonites
One	7	2	1
Two	1	0	0
None	30	35	34
Total	38	37	35

Surprisingly, the old-style Bensonites in the sample held more translocal offices than the new-style Bensonites. A possible explanation is that new-style Bensonites are not as sure they will even be in Benson next year at this time and are, therefore, less inclined to get involved.

More new- than old-style Bensonites had two or more friends in Benson political parties. The ex-Bensonites, as expected, had no friends active in nineteen cases; but in-

TABLE 21

NUMBER OF RESPONDENTS' FRIENDS IN
BENSON'S POLITICAL PARTIES

NUMBER OF FRIENDS	Old-Style	New-Style	Ex-Bensonites
One	5	4	1
Two or more	19	25	15
None	14	8	19
Total	38	37	35

Benson's Locals and Cosmopolitans

terestingly, fifteen ex-Bensonites had still maintained active friendships with Benson politicos.

To determine which group had the most friends in Benson city government, and thereby access to power and influence, an index on friends in official positions was sought in order to ascertain the power of old-style versus new-style Bensonites. The two groups were apparently equal.

Another way of isolating influence, it was believed, would be to ask respondents if they shared house visits or similar hospitality with selected influential persons (judge, doctor, pastor, lawyer, teacher, etc.). This measure—that of "influential hospitables"—is reported as follows:

Another index of status was to check identification of the preferred and most prestigious places of residence according to the views of old-style and new-style and ex-Bensonites.

The respondents were asked to name who, in their respective opinions, were the most important individuals in

TABLE 22

NUMBER OF RESPONDENTS' FRIENDS IN
BENSON'S CITY GOVERNMENT

NUMBER OF FRIENDS	Old-Style	New-Style	Ex-Bensonites
One to two	8	17	6
Three to four	6	4	2
Five or more	10	8	3
None	14	8	24
Total	38	37	35

78

TABLE 23

NUMBER OF VIP'S WITH WHOM HOSPITALITY IS SHARED

NUMBER OF VIP'S	Old-Style	New-Style	Ex-Bensonites
One	2	1	4
Two	6	4	10
Three	8	6	5
Four	20	7	3
More than four	1	15	8
None claimed	1	4	5
Total	38	37	35

TABLE 24

RESPONDENTS' OPINIONS ON BEST-PLACE-TO-LIVE

LOCATION	Old-Style	New-Style	Ex-Bensonites
Not specified	5	3	12
Northside	7	7	4
Hudson Addition	1	1	0
Southside other than Sunnyside	19	16	10
Sunnyside	6	10	9
Total	38	37	35

Benson, and the town's oldest and most prominent families. The comparative responses of the two groups varied considerably. Within each group there was remarkable consensus as to the identification of influentials and families of prestige, and there was even some agreement between old-

and new-style types. But there were also dramatic differences that far overshadowed the few names that appeared on the lists of both groups. With some exceptions, then, the generalization seems valid that old- and new-style Bensonites selected distinct sets of influentials. This is not to suggest that those persons who are leaders among the new-style group may exert the same influence with old-style types. Leadership among the old-style Bensonites, similarly, does not guarantee leadership and influence among new-style. This finding is congruent with the conclusions of most current studies that find differential "publics" in the population at large to have differential sets of leaders, and being a leader with currency in one "public" does not mean this influence is automatically transferable from one "public" to another —but instead is more likely to be confined to the particular "public" within which it negotiates influence.

6

THE
POLARIZATION
OF
BENSON'S
ECONOMY

It is now possible to explore in depth the hypothesis that lines of tension between local and translocal forces are discernible in Benson's economy. A field survey was made of Benson's economy, and an analytical survey of locals and cosmopolitans was conducted. Finally, a veritable gold mine of information about the economy was found in Benson's *Planning Reports.*

Benson is the county seat for Swift County, Minnesota. Some 90 percent of the land, 443,000 of Swift County's 478,000 acres, is given over to agricultural uses, while the statewide average proportion of county land given to agriculture in Minnesota is around 60 percent.[1] The businesses lining Benson's main streets find their primary orientation in servicing a market-oriented agriculture. Despite the increased use of automobiles and excellent highways giving farmers easy access to large centers such as Saint Cloud and Willmar, Benson's role as a trade center is secure for the immediate area.

> This farm trade territory is undergoing change, not only in the reduced size of the farm population but in purchasing habits. The mobility of our population has made it possible to patronize trading centers outside of the one within which the residence is located and business trips take farmers to other areas. However, Benson is the principal economic center for the farm trade area population and the one on which it is dependent.[2]

The primary trade belt is a thirty-mile radius around Benson, and farmers in this area trade regularly in Benson. A second trade belt, comprised of a thirty-five-mile radius, takes in farmers who trade with some regularity in Benson. And those in a third trade belt, a forty-mile radius, trade occasionally in Benson.

Sheep, hogs, cows, cattle, chickens, turkeys, corn, wheat, soybeans, flax, and barley figure high in the output for sale of farmers in the Benson area.

In 1959, Swift County raised 3,188,369 bushels of corn, 102,429 bushels of flax, and 249,804 bushels of barley.

The average Swift County farm in 1954 sold $7,122 worth of farm products, or $27.75 per acre. Total sale of farm products in Swift County in 1954 reached $12,271,923. This $12 million figure in farm sales is seen as the primary factor in the local economy in the *Planning Reports* of the Benson City Planning Commission:

TABLE 25

AGRI-PRODUCTS FOR SWIFT COUNTY, 1959

Number of sheep	13,381
Number of hogs	65,932
Number of cows	12,925
Number of cattle	35,945
Number of chickens	319,944
Number of turkeys	196,015
Bushels of corn	3,188,369
Bushels of flax	102,429
Bushels of barley	249,804

Source: *Planning Reports* (Benson, Minn.: City Planning Commission and Midwest Planning and Research, August, 1961), section on "Economic Base," p. 6.

83

The 12 million dollars in community income . . . is . . . very important. The service and sales businesses necessary to maintain this large agricultural business should increase in strength, for larger operations require more mechanization and services than smaller family farms.[3]

TRENDS IN BENSON'S AGRARIAN ECONOMY

The forces of the wider society are transforming the basic units of Benson's agrarian economy. The increasing productivity per man-hour of labor is achieved in considerable measure by increasing mechanization. The mounting costs of the investment in machinery, in turn, can be met only by increasing the scope of farm operations. In Benson, as in many areas, the number of small farms is declining.

The decreasing number of smaller farms is of concern to Bensonites, for they are aware of the consequences of tearing away of families from homesteads where for generations previously their families prospered. The rupture caused by families forced off the land in mid-twentieth century is borne out by the following statistics from Swift County on farm size. In 1949, the average size farm in Swift County was 246.5 acres, but by 1959 the average had increased to 265.7 acres. And though figures for the change from 1960 to the present are not available, knowledgeable estimates are that the period from 1960 to the present has seen an increase by an increment equal to that over the period 1949–1959. During the ten-year period from 1949 to 1959, the prototype farm showing the greatest increase was the 500- to 1,000-acre farm. In 1954, for example, there were 84 farms in this category but by 1959 the number had increased to 107.[4]

In this change, Benson shares the trends in rural areas across the nation, as documented by a survey showing a shrinkage of 20 percent in the number of small farms nationwide:

> The number of small farms across the nation shrank by more than 20 percent in the seven years between 1959 and 1966. Government farm income figures show the exodus of the little guy from the nation's farming was confined to those selling less than $10,000 worth of farm produce annually. There was an increase in larger units.[5]

An article in the *West Central Tribune* summarizes this shift in economic epicenter from many farms of small size and sales toward fewer farms of greater size and greater sales:

> The Agriculture Department's most recent farm income report shows there were 4,097,000 farms in 1959 and 3,252,000 in 1966. Farms with sales of less than $2,500 a year dropped from 1,922,000 in 1959 to 1,413,000 last year. Those with receipts of between $2,500 and $4,999 went down from 654,000 to 356,000 and those with receipts between $5,000 and $9,999 declined from 693,000 to 446,000. But farms that sold between $10,000 and $19,999 worth of farm products eased up from 503,000 to 510,000 during the seven-year period. Farms with annual sales of $20,000 and over jumped up from 325,000 to

The Polarization of Benson's Economy

527,000—an increase of 62 percent. It is this latter category that is expected to continue to make big gains at the expense of the smaller income units in the years ahead.[6]

In the Benson area in 1949, there were 1,849 farms scattered across Swift County. This number decreased to 1,723 by 1954, and by 1959 had decreased to 1,670. The ten-year period of 1949 to 1959 for Swift County showed a loss of 141 farm families. At three persons per family, this ten-year loss involved 423 people. The land vacated by these persons was swallowed up by larger farm operations. Trends in numbers and size of farms are linked with trends in acreage values and the cost of operations.[7]

According to one knowledgeable source in Benson, the acreage value of land and buildings has expanded to a point where the young man starting out in agriculture presently is increasingly dependent on credit as a substitute for actual earned income. The farmers' sons, who despite love of the rural life leave for the city, often cite debt servitude as the cause.

The increased cost of farm operations is summarized in the City Planning Commission's *Planning Reports:*

> The average value of land and buildings increased from $24,463 in 1954 to $37,572 in 1959 for an average of $13,109 per farm as compared to $12,316 increase for the state. This increase in average value can be explained in three ways, first the dollar value has inflated, second the number of farms under 50 acres has increased and many of the newly formed smaller farms have had a house and other buildings erected, third the size of the farms included are larger in acreage.[8]

86

The increased value of land and buildings on Swift County farms has followed the national inflationary spiral, rising from $24,463 in 1954 to $37,572 in 1959.[9]

THE NATIONAL FARM
ORGANIZATIONS

It has been noted that Benson's farms do not simply serve the local area but pour their products into the national economy and in securing the efficiencies necessary for successful competition follow the national trends toward mechanization and increased size. Similarly, Benson's farmers are forced to press their interests not simply in the local community, but nationally.

Farmers were among the first to seek aid from the federal government to secure credit for their operations, to improve transportation, to supply information on crop improvements and the like. The Farmers' Union (FU), the Farmers' Bureau (FB), and the National Farmers' Organization (NFO) have local branches in Benson. Since these institutions are organized nationally, each represents a recognition that the farmer—whose stereotype in our folk literature is as an autonomous personage—is collectively and nationally organized for the achievement of translocal solutions to agricultural questions.

The activity in national agricultural issues is illustrated by the following excerpt from a letter to the editor, written by a Benson farmer in response to reader criticism of an effort by members of the National Farmers' Organization to hold their milk off the market collectively in order to gain better market prices:

> This milk was only dumped after the industry refused to pay a fair price for it. This is the same principle labor uses. They offer their services or labor for a fair price, and if this cannot be gained they go on a strike. . . . once you waste an hour going on strike, it is just as hard to retrieve as milk that is being poured on the ground. I did not hear you complain about any other segments of the laboring economy striking, and I resent the fact that you picked on the one group who have not received a raise for the last 20 years. In 1947, I received $4.30 a hundred weight for Grade A milk, today in 1967, this price paid in our local area is still $4.30 a hundred weight. *Not one cent gain in 20 years.*[10]

THE TOWN'S FINANCIAL INSTITUTIONS

The fact that the rural area served by Benson shares in national trends and in part receives direct assistance from federal programs has an important effect on the town's banking institutions. An important part of the prosperity of these banks rests on their credit and financial services to the farmer. The more of such services taken over by the government, the deeper the inroads into the local banking business. Moreover the declining numbers of persons in farming has negative consequences.

The diagnosis of the City Planning Commission's *Planning Reports* acknowledges this in its prediction that a continuing decline in the number of Benson's farmers will have a detrimental effect on Benson's economic life:

> It is vitally important . . . to recall that . . . the rural population is declining and that it is expected to continue. Because Benson's economy is dependent upon retail trade and wholesaling, this will inevitably have a detrimental effect on the Benson trade area and resultant economic structure.[11]

The Swift County Bank and the First State Bank, Benson's two banks, show steady service to the financial stability of the community. As of December 31, 1965, the Swift County Bank reported assets of $8,480,742.32 and the First State Bank, $5,359,168.77. And after an interval of two years, on January 12, 1967, the Swift County Bank's assets were $8,738,122.41 and the First State Bank's assets were $5,826,864.74.[12]

The contrast of local and translocal forces in Benson's financial institutions is present in another way beyond the fact that they must compete somewhat with the federal government's financial services to farmers. The two banks are neatly split in this respect: the Swift County Bank is independent and home-owned; the First State Bank is a member bank in the "First Bank" constellation with a trans-local organization.

BENSON'S INDUSTRIES

A large number of Benson's industries serve the farmers or process agricultural products. At the time of this study some six agricultural products processing firms hired 131 men. The construction firms, too, derive much of their business from the farmers.

TABLE 26

NUMBER OF EMPLOYEES IN BENSON'S AGRI-PROCESSING FIRMS

FIRM	Number of Employees in Season
Benson Coop Creamery & Locker Plant	16
Benson Produce Co.	30
Howard's Produce	7
Lang Bluegrass	50
Munson Seed Co.	10
Benson Alfalfa Co.	18
Total	131

TABLE 27

NUMBER OF EMPLOYEES IN BENSON'S CONSTRUCTION FIRMS

FIRM	Number of Employees in Season
Anderson Ready Mix (concrete)	25
McCarthy Lumber Co.	25
Standard Lumber Co.	5
Benson Lumber Co.	4
Kleven Construction	40
Kennedy Construction	10
Total	109

Agri-Manufacturing Firms

The Dokken Machine Works in Benson builds forage box feeders and manure spreaders, and employs twenty persons. The Lorenz Machine and Manufacturing Company builds hydraulic grinders and mixers used as mobile feed mills in cattle feeding, and employs twenty-five persons. Lorenz Company also supplies farmers with parts for their machinery. Anderson Ready Mix, already listed, produces septic tanks. Pearson Brothers, a machine works, produces a mink feeder that is ridden along lines of cages and blows feed to the animals.

Larger Manufacturing

Tyler Manufacturing and Wiman Manufacturing are larger manufacturing firms in Benson; yet both manufacture products closely linked to the farm economy. Tyler produces ma-

TABLE 28

NUMBER OF EMPLOYEES IN BENSON'S MANUFACTURING FIRMS

FIRM	Number of Employees in Season
Dokken Machine Works	20
Pearson Brothers Machine	3
L. J. Benoit Co.	3
Lorenz Machine-Manufacturing	25
Tyler Manufacturing	300
Wiman Manufacturing	225

chinery that the farmer may attach to his own tractor and reduce considerably the cost of fertilizing. And Wiman produces vinyl coats and jackets. In peak employment in the winter of 1967, the Wiman plant employed 230 persons—most of them farmers' wives supplementing family income during the long winter months.

In addition, the Alfalfa Dehydration Plant employs twenty people in peak season, and is also directed to the needs of the farm economy. It serves a conservation function, as well, encouraging farmers to rebuild worn-out fields through production of alfalfa.

While the greater number of Benson's industries are tiny operations, locally owned and serving the town and surrounding countryside, it is notable that here, too, the contrast between local and translocal forces appears. The two largest manufacturing firms are under the control of absentee owners.

Trucking firms in Benson serve the farmer by hauling his goods between the local community and metropolitan markets. They also serve the local merchants.

There are a number of livestock haulers in the Benson area, who haul farmers' livestock to markets in south Saint Paul and elsewhere. United Parcel has overnight service to Benson. D and H Truck Line offers interstate and intrastate trucking out of Benson. West Central Coop offers trucking services out of its terminal in Benson, and inasmuch as its drivers are members of the Teamsters' Union this demonstrates again the intersection of Benson's local economy with translocal organization.

The railroad, which has played a prominent role in the history of Benson (as documented in an earlier chapter), continues to play an important role in Benson's economy, since Benson is on the main transcontinental line of the Great Northern Railroad with daily freight and passenger service east and west.

Benson is served by the Greyhound Bus Lines, and Greyhound cruisers run east and west through town. On Fridays, three buses run east and west—accommodating heavy use between local communities and the Twin Cities. On other days, the buses run twice each way.

Benson's Municipal Airport has a hard-surfaced runway

with a lighted field beacon, as well as hangar and gasoline facilities. Charter service is available out of this airport, but its chief use is by private pilots and their aircraft.

All of the major and a number of the minor transportation facilities of Benson are translocal in nature.

THE SERVICE INDUSTRIES

Benson has a variety of service industries, some of which are independent and home-owned, others of which are local representatives of national chains.

Within the city of Benson, 60 percent of all male em-

TABLE 29

TYPES OF SERVICE ESTABLISHMENTS IN BENSON

ESTABLISHMENT	Number
Apparel shop	6
Automotive	5
Drugstore	3
Eating and drinking	13
Grocery store	8
Furniture and appliance	6
Gasoline service station	21
Hardware and farm equipment	13
Lumber	3
Miscellaneous	11
Total	89

SMALL TOWN AND THE NATION

ployees are categorized as proprietors, officials, managers, foremen, and craftsmen. A similarly large percentage of all female employees in the city of Benson are categorized by a composite set of work roles; that is, 80 percent of the female work force is composed of clerks, sales workers, service workers, and professionals.[13] Noting that 31 percent of Benson's total labor force is composed of women, the *Planning Reports* of the City Planning Commission drew the conclusion that "a large potential exists for businesses which would find a need for hiring women."[14]

TABLE 30

NUMBER OF EMPLOYEES IN BENSON'S INDUSTRIES

INDUSTRY	Number	Percent of Total
Agriculture, forestry, fisheries residing in Benson	41	3.1
Mining	0	0
Construction	114	9.2
Manufacturing	78	6.3
Transportation, communications, and public utilities	118	9.6
Wholesale and retail trade	465	37.5
Finance, insurance, and real estate	47	3.9
Business and repair services	49	4.0
Personal services	84	6.8
Entertainment, recreation	11	.9
Professional (and related)	150	12.1
Public administration	63	5.5
Not reported	19	1.5
Total	1,239	100.0

Source: *Planning Reports,* p. 13.

In the 1950 census, 74.4 percent of Benson's population were classified as potential employees. The percentage of those over fourteen years of age actually working in 1950 was 50.2. The following two tables contain the breakdown of Bensonites at work by industry, and then an analysis of occupations in the Benson trade area.

The age at retirement is going down; the life expectancy of persons is going up; and the nuclear family of today, unlike the extended family of the old Benson, often is unlikely to include the grandparents within its own domicile. In the last decades these factors have combined to create extensive new needs for the housing of older people, and

TABLE 31

OCCUPATIONS IN BENSON, 1950

OCCUPATIONAL GROUP	Males	Females
Professional-technical	74	73
Farmers & farm managers residing in town	9	0
Managers, proprietors, and officials	173	18
Clerical	65	75
Sales workers	70	64
Foremen, craftsmen, and kindreds	203	2
Operatives	116	29
Private household workers	1	24
Service workers	34	0
Farm laborers residing in town	18	0
Laborers other than farm laborers	73	1
Occupations unreported	15	4
Total	851	388

Source: *Planning Reports*, p. 12.

SMALL TOWN AND THE NATION

Benson by its own resources could not erect the towering Park View Manor. It is at this juncture that the small town, helpless to deal with these economic problems out of its own purse, turns for help to the federal government in Washington, D.C.

A considerable segment of the population now survives on Social Security benefits. Some 2,281 residents in Swift County—the county of which Benson is county seat—were receiving some form of assistance from the Social Security Administration office as of December 31, 1966, according to the district Social Security office at nearby Marshall, Minnesota. This amounted to a total of $144,089 in Social Security assistance pumped into the local Swift County economy during 1966.[15]

We did not attempt to establish the exact proportions of Benson's labor force engaged in the work of local and translocal institutions. Nor did we seek to assess the psychological and sociological correlates of such location. Some indication of these effects, however, may be provided by the analytical survey of locals and cosmopolitans to be analyzed later.

ECONOMIC PROFILE OF THE BENSONITE

At the time of the 1960 census the median family income in Benson was $5,150.[16] In August, 1966, the local newspaper reported the findings of an economic survey of Benson.[17]

97

Though this was far from its intention, the survey provides evidence of additional aspects of the intersection of local and translocal forces in Benson's economic life.

There are 1,048 houses in the city limits of Benson, and at the time of the survey only six were vacant, and eleven new residences were under construction. One of the impressions the visitor gets of Benson is that the local citizens there are "homing types" and this impression is backed up by the fact that 90 percent of city residential structures are private homes, and only 9 percent are apartments. The remaining 1 percent of Benson's structures is comprised of businesses and service places.

Further analysis of community housing reveals that 57 percent of all Bensonites own their own private homes. Twenty-three percent of all Benson's citizens are presently working toward home ownership by currently paying on a mortgage. And 16 percent of all Bensonites are now renting. The social space ratio in Benson is 5.8 rooms per home on the average, and there is an average of 3.4 people per Benson family. For transportation, there is an average of 1.9 automobiles per family.

Seventy-three percent of Benson's families have at least one member employed, although 26 percent of the families of Benson also have at least one member retired.

Six percent of Benson's labor force is employed in other communities during the day (most typically, Willmar) —driving to work there and returning in the evenings for domicile in Benson. This finding again dramatizes the cleavage apparent between the economic locus of the Bensonite

SMALL TOWN AND THE NATION

in his traditional local setting versus the translocal regional forces. A not unusual pattern for some unskilled workers is to hold a job in a neighboring town like Willmar for long enough to save up a "nest egg" and then quit the job for a respite at home again in Benson.

With respect to the length of stay of Benson's residents in their current homes, 47 percent of the families have lived in their present homes for less than ten years. But 44 percent have lived in their current homes for longer than ten years. A certain contentment with family life in Benson is characteristically revealed by the fact that 91.4 percent of the families—when interviewed—expressed plans to remain housed in their present homes.

The survey further found that 99.5 percent of the families buy their groceries in Benson, that 99.4 percent of the families buy their hardware in Benson, that 80 percent buy their clothes in Benson, and that 99.3 percent purchase their drugs in Benson.

In response to a question as to whether Benson lacked a variety of goods from which the consumer might select, there is evidence again of the cleavage. To the question, "Does Benson lack variety in goods you wish to purchase?", 37.1 percent replied in the affirmative, documenting the way in which the present-day Bensonite's economic loyalties are divided in collective consumer-buying habits between the realm of local goods and services and those offered by translocal economic configurations. It should be noted, however, that some 60 percent answered in the negative, inferring thereby that Benson's local stores offer a sufficient variety of consumer goods for their purchase. Only 2.9 percent of those interviewed failed to have an opinion on the question, or otherwise failed to answer.

Some 84 percent of those interviewed thought that Benson's business district was modern enough the way it stands. Nevertheless, 77 percent of this same group favored more modernization.

And finally, the further breakdown of where Bensonites shopped when they could not find satisfaction in Benson is as follows: of the 20 percent who said they bought clothing outside of Benson, 5.4 percent said they made purchases by mail-order; 7.3 percent made shopping trips to the Twin Cities; 4.6 percent to nearby Willmar; 1.2 percent to nearby Montevideo; and 0.7 percent to some other translocal center. *

FINDINGS OF THE ANALYTICAL SURVEY

Data from our field survey and the rich materials of Benson's *Planning Reports* and information provided in her newspaper establish beyond any question the existence of a polarization between local and translocal forces in every area of her economic life: in the farms, in the banking institutions, in the industrial and service institutions, in her labor force. The purpose of the analytical survey of old- and new-

* Although some of the interpretations given the survey's findings are those of the present researchers, the basis for them is anchored in the findings as reported in the local newspaper.

style Bensonites was not to establish the existence of the polarization but to explore the extent to which it is possible to quantitatively establish this contrast and its effects. Scales of localism and cosmopolitanism were designed with respect to a series of selected economic characteristics and economic attitudes. It was theorized that the average scores on the scale by old-style Bensonites would be weighted toward localism; the average scores of new-style Bensonites would be weighted toward cosmopolitanism. A group of ex-Bensonites, serving as a control group, was expected to differ from both experimental groups.

The Economic Characteristics of Old- and New-Style Bensonites

A total of nine questions (questionnaire items 7–15) were asked with regard to economic characteristics. These included type of occupation, amount of income, value of tools, receipt of old-age assistance, ownership of business, the value of home owned, ownership of selected properties, number of cars owned, and the amount of rent paid if renting. The response to these items was scored on a scale from 1 to 7 in such manner that the higher the score the greater the cosmopolitanism, the lower the score the greater the localism. It was, of course, generally theorized that old-style Bensonites would earn lower mean scores than would new-style Bensonites.

If one combines the two samples and calculates the total group mean score, the distribution of scores of the individuals in the subgroups around the total group mean score may be tested by chi-square. If the number of scores

101

TABLE 32

SELECTED ECONOMIC CHARACTERISTICS OF
OLD- AND NEW-STYLE BENSONITES

| CHARACTERISTIC | Mean Scale Scores | | Predicted |
	Old-Style	New-Style	
Type of occupation	3.60	5.2	Yes
Amount of income	2.81	2.86	Yes
Value of tools	3.65	3.29	No
Old-age assistance	5.73	7.00	Yes
Ownership of business	3.68	1.70	No
Value of home owned	3.18	2.64	No
Ownership of selected properties	2.34	2.35	Yes
Number of cars	3.60	3.43	No
Monthly rent	1.13	1.81	Yes

of a given quality found in a subsample could be anticipated on the basis of chance alone only 5 percent of the time, one may reject the null-hypothesis that there is no significant difference between the sample groups relating to the particular characteristic.

On five of the nine economic characteristics on which it was predicted that old-style and new-style Bensonites would differ, the means of the two groups differed in the expected direction. On five of the nine traits (though somewhat different from those on which the means were in the expected direction), the two groups were significantly different on the chi-square at the 5 percent or 1 percent level. On two other traits the differences were significant at the 10 percent level. On only two traits, ownership of business and value of home owned, were the two groups not only the reverse

SMALL TOWN AND THE NATION

TABLE 33

SELECTED ECONOMIC CHARACTERISTICS OF
OLD- AND NEW-STYLE BENSONITES

CHARACTERISTIC	Chi-Square Test of Score Distribution	Significance[a]
Type of occupation	3.00	NS[b]
Amount of income	1.29	NS
Value of tools	1.11	NS
Old-age assistance	6.65	.01
Ownership of business	8.06	.01
Value of home owned	3.33	.05
Ownership of selected properties	6.42	.01
Number of cars	2.83	NS
Monthly rent	7.4	.01

[a] At one degree of freedom.
[b] NS = not significant.

of expected but significantly so. This could very well have been due to a mistaken expectation that led us to underestimate the extent of professionalism among new-style Bensonites and the extent to which they may be disinclined to invest in expensive home properties. However this may be, there is no doubt that the two groups possess different economic characteristics.

The Economic Attitudes of Old-and New-Style Bensonites

A total of twelve statements were offered to the samples of Bensonites to which they were able to respond with varying degrees of agreement or disagreement. These statements were scored in such a manner that low scores would indicate a preference for the local orientation of the economy and high scores would indicate receptivity to translocal economic orientations. In the same manner as with economic characteristics it is possible to compare the mean scores of the two

TABLE 34

ECONOMIC ATTITUDES OF OLD- AND NEW-STYLE BENSONITES

STATEMENT	Mean Scores		
	Old-Style	New-Style	Predicted
The control of local Benson businesses by outsiders is not a bad thing	1.13	1.81	Yes
People living in Benson should buy locally	3.68	2.94	No
Corporations should take over all farms	3.10	3.27	Yes
Benson firms should be locally owned	1.94	1.91	No
The family farm is the backbone of the nation	1.52	1.21	No
Most Benson workers are underpaid	3.36	3.91	Yes
The family homestead should be kept in the family	2.94	3.43	Yes
Benson farmers should sell out to wildlife refuges	3.78	5.21	Yes
Land is the most important source of wealth	2.94	3.48	Yes
The more land a man owns the better off he is	6.15	6.24	Yes
Farmers are not paid enough	4.84	5.00	Yes
One should leave for a better job even if one is happier in Benson	2.26	2.62	Yes

groups and to examine the chi-squares of the distribution of the sample scores around the group mean. The following two tables summarize the findings:

The contrast between the attitudes of old- and new-style Bensonites is even more striking than the contrast in their economic characteristics. This, perhaps, is to be expected; for in a tiny town of a mere 4,000, both groups make a living

TABLE 35

DISTRIBUTION OF ATTITUDE SCORES OF
OLD- AND NEW-STYLE BENSONITES

STATEMENT	Chi-Squares	Significance[a]
The control of local Benson businesses by outsiders is not a bad thing	7.0589	.01
People living in Benson should buy locally	5.8985	.02
Corporations should take over all farms	6.6679	.01
Benson firms should be locally owned	4.4018	.05
The family farm is the backbone of the nation	6.6974	.01
Most Benson workers are underpaid	2.9338	NS[b]
The family homestead should be kept in the family	5.1488	.05
Benson farmers should sell out to wildlife refuges	8.555	.01
Land is the most important source of wealth	3.3339	NS
The more land a man owns, the better off he is	1.0751	NS
Farmers are not paid enough	1.2754	NS
One should leave for a better job even if one is happier in Benson	8.0681	.01

[a] At one degree of freedom.
[b] NS = not significant.

in much the same way. However, their social psychologies are sharply distinct. In all but three of the economic attitudes the two groups differed in the way predicted in advance. On all but four items the differences were significant at the 5 percent level or better. In two other instances the differences approached significance, being significant at the .10 level.

A reanalysis of the attitudes on which the expected differences did not appear would perhaps show the presence of intervening factors. However, it is quite unnecessary to advance ad hoc arguments to conclude that two distinct social psychological worlds have been established by the analytical survey.

Bensonites and Ex-Bensonites

At the time the samples of old- and new-style Bensonites were drawn, it was also deemed advisable to gather samples of persons born and reared in Benson who had left the community. If the reflections on localism and cosmopolitanism were correct, such ex-Bensonites should represent cosmopolitan types. On the other hand, comparisons with new-style Bensonites would very probably not show the same contrasts, for they were anticipated to be the more cosmopolitan group of resident Bensonites.

When old-style Bensonites were compared with ex-Bensonites, ex-Bensonites as expected were much more cosmopolitan both in characteristics and attitudes. Some surprises were in store, however, when new-style and ex-Bensonites were compared. Although there was less difference between the two groups than between old-style and ex-Bensonites, the ex-Bensonites were somewhat more cosmopolitan than both groups.

It is unnecessary to burden the text with relevant tables. They are available for perusal, however, in the appendix. The control group strongly reinforced the findings with respect to the experimental groups.

The Ambivalence of Benson's Economy

There is still the Bensonite who buys all those things he deems necessary for life in Benson and whose work or other economic activity takes place largely within the framework of the traditional economy. But there is another side to Benson's present economy of which even the most tradition-bound Bensonite is acutely aware. The point of gravity in this other aspect of Benson's economy is located in the world outside.

The effect of translocal forces on the economy is epitomized by Park View Manor, the federally financed housing project for older persons. It could not have been constructed without outside federal assistance. Regulations of the federal government in considerable measure determine who is able to benefit by its facilities. While its benefits are beyond question and necessary, the project is a reminder that the local economy is no longer completely able to care for its older people, at least in a manner that everyone agrees they deserve. The editor of the *Swift County Monitor* dealt directly with this problem in an editorial:

> Low-rent housing for the elderly in Benson has just one justification—it will give men and women who have been

good citizens of this nation for many years a place in which they can live in dignity and comfort which is within their limited means. There will be 70 apartments occupied in Benson by people who earn less than $3,200 a year and have less than $10,000 in assets. If the richest nation in the world can't do at least this for those senior citizens who can enjoy this type of housing, then, indeed, we have betrayed the free enterprise system, turned it into a cold, unfeeling monster. As to the fear of not getting some of our tax dollars in Benson, it's only common sense that we, who have never profited by defense industries or other government activity and have fought to keep our heads above water while farmers are subsidizing the rest of the nation, should battle to gain some return. . . . Those who cry "socialism" today are of the same thinking as those who fought public schools, social security, the formation of unions, rules to control monopolies, to regulate stock and commodity market tradings, public roads, and all the rest. For a free enterprise system to flourish there must be equality of opportunity, and government must do for the society what it can't do individually.[18]

As we have seen, a confrontation of local and translocal forces occurs at every point in Benson's economy. It is most fundamentally a farm service economy and the productivity of its farms can be seen as providing the motor power to almost everything else. But the basic agrarian economy is caught up with national trends. Increasing mechanization and larger farms are reducing the number of farms and driving families off the land. Federal government programs and subsidies bypass the service economy and directly affect the farmer. The farmers, in turn, join the national farm organizations to lobby for their interests at all levels of government and to promote their interests in national and inter-

108

national farm markets. The local service community, in short, is less and less the sole factor in the lives of the farmers as time goes by.

The transformation of the agrarian economy by forces in the national community encourages various penetrations of the service community by other translocal forces. Local industry services the farmers by processing products and by supplying them with various materials and equipment. As farmers are pressed off the land into the towns, they may form local enclaves of labor that may be exploited more cheaply than the labor of the larger urban centers by translocal industrial concerns. Hence a confrontation occurs between local and translocal industries at this level.

It has been noted that in the local financial institutions a confrontation again occurs between a locally owned, independent bank and a bank that is the local representative of a chain of banks.

The local service industries, too, divide between locally owned and operated independents (such as Wigfield's) and the member of the chain (such as the Ward's Catalogue store).

Benson's transportation facilities also break down between the locally owned and operated and the translocal.

Benson's labor force divides between those who make a living by service in locally owned independent industries and services and those who make a living in service of various translocal institutions. Included in the latter category are those local residents whose resources come largely from federal government projects or programs such as Social Security, Medicare and the like, and those younger people who earn a living in the Neighborhood Youth Corps (known in Benson as the Little Crow Community Council).

Our theory that these two sets of forces in Benson's economy would be manifested in contrasting styles of life as between samples of old-style and new-style Bensonites proved to be correct.

NOTES

1. *Planning Reports* (Benson, Minn.: City Planning Commission and Midwest Planning and Research, August, 1961), section on "Economic Base," p. 5.

2. *Ibid.*

3. *Ibid.*, p. 6.

4. *Ibid.*, p. 5.

5. *West Central* (Willmar, Minn.) *Tribune*, August 14, 1967, p. 1.

6. *Ibid.*

7. *Planning Reports*, p. 4.

8. *Ibid.*, pp. 5–6.

9. *Ibid.*, p. 6.

10. John Minor, quoted in *West Central* (Willmar, Minn.) *Tribune*, April 28, 1967, "Letters to the Editor," p. 4.

SMALL TOWN AND THE NATION

11. *Planning Reports,* p. 14.

12. *Swift County* (Minn.) *Monitor,* January 12, 1967, p. 4.

13. *Planning Reports,* p. 15.

14. *Ibid.,* p. 13.

15. *Swift County* (Minn.) *Monitor,* June 8, 1967, p. 1.

16. Benson Chamber of Commerce.

17. *Swift County* (Minn.) *Monitor,* August 25, 1966, pp. 1–4.

18. Ronald Anfinson, *Swift County Monitor,* editorial reprinted in the *Minneapolis Tribune,* July 7, 1967, p. 4.

7

CONFLICTING
STYLES
OF
SOCIALIZATION

Socialization is the process by which individuals are transformed into full-fledged social beings. Socialization is a pervasive process, continuing from birth to death; however, there are phases during which the activities of special institutions of socialization dominate the life of a person. One such is schooling, the deliberate attempt to shape the learning and behavior of persons. Another aspect of socialization is church life. Health and welfare institutions represent a third.

Institutions of socialization tend to remain local in scope long after the institutions of wealth and power have become translocal in orientation. Education, religion, health, and welfare are typically a jealously guarded prerogative of primary groups. Even in the face of growing need, many Americans are hesitant about federal aid to education lest their control over it slip away. They are concerned to keep politics and religion separate. Only after World War II were Americans willing to accept Medicare.

However, while the institutions of socialization tend to remain local in orientation, the problems of socialization are posed by the society as a whole.

An individual must acquire the personality resources that permit him to cope with his world or he may crumble when the going is rough. His education must include the knowledge and skills that enable him to deal effectively with his economic and political problems. His religion is addressed to the meaning of life, but the meaning of life is dependent on the individual's total social condition and not simply on his primary groups. The individual's health and welfare are affected by the individual's total economic and political situation, as he may realize when his air and water are polluted by modern industry or his health is threatened by the testing of atomic weapons. In all such situations, translocal forces may affect the sphere of socialization.

For all of these reasons, the second of our major hypotheses was that major lines of stress from the conflict of local and nonlocal interests appear in Benson's institutions of socialization. For the verification of this hypothesis, a field survey was conducted involving extensive interviews of responsible citizens. A variety of local materials such as reports by institutional, personal, and newspaper accounts were assembled. Finally a number of questions on socialization characteristics and attitudes were posed to the samples of Bensonites and ex-Bensonites who completed our analytical survey.

EDUCATION IN BENSON

Benson's educational institutions include the public schools in town, the Saint Francis Parochial School (grades one through eight only), and a remnant of twelve ungraded schools in Benson's immediate vicinity. The educational horizon of the Bensonite is also strongly affected by the presence in nearby towns of a state college and a branch of the University of Minnesota.

The most immediate way in which the problem of localism-translocalism appears for Benson's educational systems is in the conflict over the orientation of the educational enterprise: whether it should be primarily directed to the needs of the local community or to the success of young people in the world at large. To direct education to the first may enhance the local community at the expense of

114

those who migrate; to direct education to the second requirement may be to build in a mechanism that tends to pump the finest intelligence and talent of local young people into the world at large.

Benson's Public Schools

Benson's public school system is the largest in Swift County, and is housed in the Southside and Northside Elementary School buildings; in the Northside Junior High School building; and in the Northside Senior High School building. Nearly one hundred teachers are on the payroll of the public schools, which includes seventeen teachers on the staff of the Northside Elementary School, ten teachers on the faculty at the Southside Elementary School, twenty-six on the senior high teaching staff, thirty on the faculty of the junior high, a superintendent of schools, a senior high principal, a junior high principal, an athletic director, a school nurse, six office secretaries, sixteen bus drivers, ten custodians, thirteen school-lunch cooks, and four library clerks.

The Benson public schools also offer full schedules of lyceum programs, forensics, music clubs, science clubs, patrolmen on duty for Northside Elementary, remedial reading programs, psychological programs, part-time school doctor, full-time school nurse, lighted football field, modern fleet of school buses to reach into the hinterlands for students, noon hot-lunch programs in all its branches, approved driver's training education, and complete kindergarten program.

The board of education is composed of seven members: a chairman, vice-chairman, clerk, treasurer, and three directors. These are popularly elected in the Benson school district's jurisdiction. School board elections are no pushover, with many hotly contested races on record.

Saint Francis Parochial

This school, with grades one through eight, is operated under the auspices of the Saint Francis Roman Catholic Church in Benson. As of 1967, it had a faculty of ten, consisting of seven nuns, the parish priest, and two lay persons. It has an enrollment of 176 pupils.

The Remaining Rural Schools

When school bells sounded the opening of the 1967 school year, there were still twelve ungraded rural schools remaining scattered in the countryside and smaller towns in Benson's immediate vicinity—all under their own school boards, elected by farmers or townsmen in the neighborhood. These remain under the supervision, also, of the Swift County superintendent of schools,* an official elected from countywide balloting. Scores of other white-painted, one-room schools that once dotted the Benson countryside are closed, with doors locked—their students now sent into Benson.

The Philosophy of Benson's Public Schools

In 1948 the Benson public schools adopted a formal and written statement of the philosophy upon which is based

---

* Since the study was completed, rural schools have been placed under the town superintendents of schools.

SMALL TOWN AND THE NATION

TABLE 36

ENROLLMENTS IN BENSON'S EDUCATIONAL INSTITUTIONS, 1967

SCHOOL	Grades	Enrollment
Benson public	1–6	685
Saint Francis parochial	1–8	176
Benson public	7–12	1,036
Total		1,897

Source: Field interviews.

their attempts to educate the youth of the community. The formulation was arrived at through the coordinated effort of the board of education, the faculty, and the PTA, and is presently included in the notebook of information given to new faculty members.

The ideals of the small town with strong local orientations dominate the statement. The ideas expressed are strongly democratic in the spirit of town-meeting democracy, emphasizing that regardless of a youth's socio-economic status, ethnicity, mental or physical ability, he should have access to a suitable education.[1] The statement is strongly normative. "Major considerations in the educational program must be given to the development of acceptable behavior patterns which are evidenced by attitudes, appreciations, understandings, and abilities."[2] The statement insists that education should extend over the whole range of life, emphasizing practicality, common decency, individualism, social responsibility, and democracy. The curriculum includes all educative experiences of the individual under the direc-

Conflicting Styles of Socialization

tion or supervision of the school. "Learning is most effective when the learning situation is purposeful and meaningful to the learner."[3] The school program must provide certain common learnings, minimum essentials, the common knowledge and skills that are needed by all persons in normal living, it states.

> . . . it has meaning only as it contributes directly to desirable patterns of behavior. The school must be concerned with the education of the whole individual; that is, with physical, intellectual, emotional, social, and ethical development. The school program must therefore provide a curriculum which will assure continuous growth toward a well-rounded individual. . . .
>
> Each individual should be given opportunities for experiences in which he can be successful in some significant part of the school program. The school must give each individual a sense of belonging; of being wanted and appreciated. . . . The school program should stimulate individuals and encourage them to continue the pursuit of their community interests.[4]

The philosophy of education formulated for Benson's public schools is primarily oriented toward fitting the individual as a responsible member of a small local community. However, the statement with which the formulators of this philosophy of education conclude sounds as if its authors had a wary eye over their shoulders. "The curriculum must be alive and flexible in order to meet the needs of youth who are living in a changing world."[5]

Benson's educators have a keen realization of the fact that a considerable proportion of their young people will have to leave Benson and make their way in the world out-

SMALL TOWN AND THE NATION

side. In adjusting realistically to this possibility the curriculum is also designed to prepare students for the university or for various professional schools.

They would like to believe that the ideals of the primary group, as Cooley would have described them, which dominate their philosophy of education, also constitute the ideal preparation for life in the outside world. They know, however, that this is not entirely the case. In Benson, the individual primarily deals with people he has known all his life. In the large metropolitan center he deals largely with strangers. In Benson, interpersonal judgments are based largely on detailed knowledge of the individual and of his family; in the large metropolitan center, interpersonal judgment is based largely on the external forms and trappings of social roles. In Benson, individuals are valued for their character; in the large metropolitan center, "character" refers to that idiosyncratic property of intransigent individualism that so often stands in the way of using the individual as an interchangeable part in the social machine. In Benson, the individual who pretends to be what he is not is a four-flusher; in the metropolitan center, survival often depends on the clever management of impressions. Many Bensonites in their hearts suspect that all the vices of Benson are the virtues of the metropolis, and cheating, lying, and dissembling carried to the level of high art are the keys to success in the great world outside. And yet this is the world that a considerable portion of Benson's youth must face. Hence, after carefully enumerating the primary group virtues one by one as educational objectives, they end their formulation with a reference to the changing needs of youth.

The board of education is selected by popular election. It hires a school administration—and through this leadership the Benson public schools are administered. The superintendent, hired by the board, is paid to assume responsibility, to hire a professional staff of teachers, cooks for the cafeteria, janitors, bus drivers, and others.

Here again one encounters the tension that exists between decisions that are purely local and those, though affecting local life, that are made outside Benson. For example, the standards for high school instruction and accreditation are made outside of Benson's city limits at the state board of education. There are, as another illustration, state conventions for school board members at which they come into direct confrontation with translocal organization. The board of education, acknowledging its debt to schools outside of Benson in formulating Benson's policy, states: "A word of thanks to the many schools whose manual of policies were studied and used as the basic pattern for this."[6]

Other Manifestations of Translocalism

Among the teachers there is a group that tend to settle and become themselves socialized into Benson's community life as "natives"—owning a home, making additional lifetime investments in Benson, and becoming fixtures in local institutional life in areas other than education even while they keep their teaching positions. There is another group of teachers who for various reasons are less likely to settle into Benson's life. This latter group has usually taught fewer years. Moreover, members of this group tend to spend weekends away from Benson, perhaps in the Twin Cities, and they are more likely to rent rather than buy a home.

Programs administered by the teachers also reflect in part local and translocal forces. Some teachers function in the traditional graded classroom which has always been a part of the local budgetary provisions; on the other hand, a special staff member may be hired to teach a program in remedial reading, in which case funds may come from the federal government.

An illustration of the national origin of one program in Benson's local institutions of socialization is its "Operation Headstart." This program, passed as a part of Lyndon B. Johnson's national legislative program, allocated funds for classroom instruction on the local level, and its announcement serves as an explanation:

> Headstart Classes
> Will start June 12.
> Project Headstart, directed by the Little Crow Community Council, Inc., is currently registering pupils to be enrolled in its summer school program. Classroom instruction of this program will begin officially Monday, June 12, at four sites: Appleton, Benson, Willmar and Villard. Social service personnel are presently contacting families in these communities to enroll pre-kindergarten children in the program. Parents contacted are urged to make every effort to allow their children to attend the program. Project Headstart is organized around a daily classroom activity. The program will provide student transportation, health services, a noon meal, and other social services important to the development of these children.[7]

Headstart exemplifies the federally financed educational program carried on at the local level.

The American Field Service program of placing a foreign-exchange student in the local Benson public school is yet another indication of the confrontation in Benson's socialization institutions between the local community and extralocal organization. It is unlikely that Benson would or could alone, without the auspices of some national-international organization such as the American Field Service, secure a foreign-exchange student for the Benson public school. Money to finance the program, though, is raised on the local level in Benson, and, in addition, a Bensonite consents to open his own home as an "American parent" to the foreign student—thus it is not purely a case of the initiative and power of the translocal organization. But without the organizational web of translocal organization, it is doubtful that the program could be brought to Benson.

The local PTA chapter in Benson participates in the Minnesota state and national PTA organization, and in the 1967 school year—for example—many specialists were brought in from outside Benson to share their expertise with interested Bensonites. One such example is in sex education which, during some more traditional moment in Benson's biography, might not have been subjected to such an open discussion. But in the 1967 school year, a chaplain at the Minnesota Home School in nearby Sauk Centre was brought to Benson where he presented a lecture on sex education to parents and teachers at a public meeting.[8]

BEA

The teachers in Benson public schools are organized in a local branch of the Minnesota Education Association (MEA) and are known as the BEA. They meet regularly during the school year, have an assignment schedule for committees (typically one teacher serves on one committee on some aspect of school affairs). Total cost of professional dues in 1966–1967 school year was $39 per teacher, and this included the $10 National Education Association fee, the MEA dues of $25, and the BEA dues of $4; again this intersection of national interests (NEA dues) and state interests (MEA dues) comes into play with the more locally oriented BEA.

Among the committees are: one to give assistance to the new teacher, the Big Brother Committee; a political action committee for educators (PACE) concerned with national and state legislation bearing on education; and the grievance committee. The grievance committee usually takes up matters confined to the local school; the scope of PACE is necessarily with political affairs largely translocal in nature.

Future Plans of Benson High School Graduates

The future plans of Benson high school graduates show, again, the cleavage between local and nonlocal interests.

Of the graduating seniors in the spring of 1967, the following shows the breakdown as to their future plans: thirty-one planned on attending a public college or university; twenty-six planned on attending a private college or university; thirty-nine planned on matriculating at various vocational-technical schools; eighteen planned immediate work in the labor force; thirteen planned immediate enlistment into the armed forces; ten planned on attending schools of nursing; and an additional eight planned to go to college but had not yet made definite plans. Seven said they could go on to junior colleges. Eight said they would attend a business college or other trade school. Two members of the class were noncommital, and nine failed to respond to the counselor's survey.[9]

The more specialized one's college or university training, the less likely one is to find a niche in Benson. Graduates of schools of business administration by and large work for national corporations and are transferred from metropolis to metropolis where firms have their branches. Benson hires only about a hundred teachers, and those Benson graduates who become teachers generally will not return to Benson to teach. Those Benson young people, on the other hand, who go into the labor force immediately, perhaps with a Benson firm such as Tylers, tend to settle into Benson's community life as permanent local citizens.

Benson's most valuable product, its youth, is also Benson's most valuable export.

CHURCH LIFE IN BENSON

Above the church listings in the *Swift County Monitor* is the caption: "Attend and support the church of your choice regularly." Benson has two types of churches: the one located on the fringes of the city, and the one in the city. Table 37 shows church membership totals for Benson's nine community churches (within city limits).

TABLE 37

BENSON'S CHURCH MEMBERSHIP TOTALS

CHURCH	Total Membership
Our Redeemer's Lutheran	2,330
Trinity Lutheran	300
Saint Mark's Lutheran	500
Saint Francis Catholic	1,015
Christ Episcopal	20
Pilgrim Congregational	300
Assembly of God	26
First Baptist	121
First Evangelical Free	35

Source: Field interviews.

Benson's nine community churches show a total membership that is greater than Benson's current population. The reasons for this are threefold:

Many farmers residing on the countryside around Benson have held membership in Benson churches for many years, and while they would not be counted in Benson's city population, they are on the church rolls in city churches.

A number of ex-Bensonites who have moved elsewhere nevertheless keep their church membership "at home" in Benson.

Finally, many farmers and their families, who used to hold memberships in many rural churches that once flourished on Benson's city limits, now have moved their memberships into Benson's city churches inasmuch as their old rural parishes have been disbanded. One of these, the Lake Hazel Rural Lutheran Church, was disbanded on July 1, 1967; its fate at the hands of twentieth-century social forces is examined later.

Of the 4,647 members listed on the rolls of Benson's community churches, 3,130 belong to the three Lutheran churches inside Benson's city limits.

Our Redeemer's Lutheran Church

Benson's largest church, Our Redeemer's Lutheran Church, conducts two Sunday morning worship services, carries broadcasts on KBMO Radio, has a regular church newspaper sent to members and friends, has two full-time pastors and a visitation pastor, and has the largest budget of any church in town. In May of 1967, it paid out $2,525 in salaries for that month alone.[10]

The confirmation, a stringent two-year course conducted by the Lutheran pastor, is one of the keynotes of Our Redeemer's Lutheran Church's socialization of its youth. Weekly classes are held in this confirmation, and students are expected to give effort equal to secular school lessons. Historically in the parish, the course is climaxed by a public examination period at which time the prospective confirmands face their parents, their pastor-teacher, and the public to answer questions regarding the Faith. At confirmation time, they are called upon to confirm the decision that was made for them years earlier at their baptism. And following this, they receive their first sacrament of Holy Communion.

It is an event attended by relatives who often travel great distances to take part. The service itself constitutes a serious and devout moment in the socialization process.

While its confirmation and ritual retain much of the traditional religious meaning, Our Redeemer's Lutheran Church also illustrates the new church that has emerged in small towns as a result of consolidating forces. Our Redeemer's is the result of the merger of two early local churches—Our Saviour's and Immanuel. For the fiscal year 1967, the new Our Redeemer's Church had a budget of $88,123; this was made possible only by the concentration of resources which earlier had been autonomous.

Table 38 shows the 1966 and the 1967 budgets of the church.

The organizational units of Our Redeemer's Lutheran Church budget show the influence of both local and translocal interests. Substantial budgetary items go to the Lutheran synodical organization itself, as well as to the district church office, while other substantial items go to the payment of local salaries, local provisions, and local activities.

Our Redeemer's Church utilizes a most modern organizational network to conduct its socialization activities in worship, Christian education, and service. Formal committees, groups, and boards of the church in 1967 included: the ushers' club, the young adults club, the department of Sunday school superintendents, the Sunday school department itself, the Scouts, the organists, the adult advisers to the Luther League, the junior and senior Luther Leagues, the library board, the Ladies Aid fellowship (a local branch of

TABLE 38

OUR REDEEMER'S LUTHERAN CHURCH BUDGET, 1966 AND 1967

EXPENDITURE	1966	1967
Gideon Society	$ 100.00	$ 100.00
Lutheran Student Fund	300.00	300.00
Zion Society for Israel	50.00	50.00
Book Mission	25.00	25.00
Seamen's Mission	25.00	25.00
Mission Family Support	3,000.00	3,000.00
Native Pastor scholarship	350.00	350.00
Synodical budget	16,640.00	16,640.00
United Temperance Society	50.00	50.00
District budget	4,230.00	4,689.00
Lac Qui Parle conference	160.00	160.00
Bible Camp support	400.00	400.00
American Bible Society	100.00	100.00
Pastor Sucher's salary	8,200.00	8,200.00
Pastor Bervig's salary	7,500.00	8,000.00
Pensions	2,166.00	2,235.60
Secretary-treasurer's salary	4,080.00	4,080.00
Secretary's salary	2,280.00	2,280.00
Organist's salary	600.00	600.00
Music director's salary	450.00	450.00
Junior choir director's salary	300.00	300.00
Cherub choir director's salary	300.00	300.00
Youth choir director's salary	400.00	400.00
Music clinics	50.00	50.00
Vacation Bible school	325.00	200.00
Bible campers' support	100.00	100.00
Librarian's salary	200.00	200.00
Library book fund	1,500.00	1,000.00
Postage	400.00	450.00
Supplies	2,500.00	2,690.00
Organ contract	150.00	150.00
Choir gown upkeep	100.00	100.00

128

TABLE 38 (continued)

EXPENDITURE	1966	1967
Church paper	500.00	635.00
Debt retirement on church	11,772.00	11,772.00
Debt retirement on parsonage	1,980.00	1,980.00
Debt retirement on parsonage	(a)	600.00
Insurance	1,673.00	1,825.72
Custodian salary	4,880.00	4,880.00
Fuel	3,000.00	2,800.00
Utilities	1,700.00	1,925.00
Social Security	485.00	550.00
Equipment and repair	500.00	450.00
Real estate repair	1,000.00	500.00
Church higher education	1,100.00	1,080.00
KBMO Radio	1,080.00	1,080.00
Total	**$87,052.41**	**$88,123.56**

Source: Our Redeemer's Lutheran Church Directory and Budget Sheet, 1967.
[a] Figures missing from source.

a national group, American Lutheran Church Women), the Sunday Night Fellowship, choir directors, the altar guild, the board of deacons, the board of education, the cemetery committee, the church and parsonage committee, the stewardship committee, the collection committee, the committee for Every Member Visitation, and other organizational units as well.

The new Our Redeemer's Lutheran Church has replaced the old Our Saviour's and Immanuel churches, and even the synodical change that has occurred in the course of the transformation is significant. The Our Saviour's and Immanuel churches of old were members of the old ELC synod

(Evangelical Lutheran Church). But in its new building, the merged congregation is itself a member of a new, merged and more consolidated larger synodical organization, the American Lutheran Church. The trends in Benson's eight other churches are very similar to those in Our Redeemer's Church.

The Fate of the Older Religious Pattern

The Lake Hazel Rural Lutheran parish typifies the older religious localism that is now surrendering to nonlocal forces in Benson's life.

In 1871, forty Norwegian immigrants to the New World gathered at the shores of Lake Hazel, under some of the trees that line its banks, and founded a church. The language used in its early services was Norwegian.

On July 24, 1871, the Lake Hazel church fathers held their first sacrament of baptism, with the baptism that day of Peder Pederson, the son of Ole Andreas and Guri Svensen Pederson. Peder Pederson—the infant who was baptized to mark the church's first baptism—spanned in his own biography almost the complete life-span of his church. Peder Pederson died in 1947, only twenty years before the Lake Hazel Church's abandonment.

During the church's first sixteen years, the pioneers conducted their public worship services in homes that surrounded their little "Norwegian lake." Originally they used a schoolhouse near the lake for a house of worship, and at times they gathered under the willows around the lake to worship and sing praises to their God. The Norwegian

130

"Klokker"* (leader in sacred songs) would wave his arms dramatically to lead them in the collective singing of their familiar favorite: *"Den Store Hvide Flok,"* and other Norwegian hymns.

Once a beehive of ecclesiastical activity for a wide area of Benson's immediate northern fringe, the Lake Hazel Lutheran Church had an early Ladies Aid organization that was, ironically, founded by a man. The story is one of the pearls of folklore of the area. In 1884, Lars Bagstad was on a visit to North Dakota and while there observed a Ladies Aid group making great organized contributions to the educational life of the parish; he was so impressed that he brought the formula home with him where he organized the Lake Hazel Ladies Aid.**

The church building was erected in 1887 on a high point overlooking the waters of the lake on the space which is now the church's cemetery. When, in 1924, the church building was moved across the road, it left room for the cemetery. It was at this time that a basement was added. As late as 1949, the congregation still flourished, at which time the church members spent $15,000 to remodel the church building. But throughout the 1950s, it became increasingly harder to get and keep a pastor. In the early 1960s the church fathers began to experience redoubled

* Ole Andreas Pederson, Klokker, is the great-grandfather of one of the coauthors, Galen Hanson.
** Mrs. Anna Torgerson, eighty-eight years old, who has been a member of the Lake Hazel Lutheran Church for more than sixty years, provided data upon which much of the foregoing analysis was based. Mildred Torgerson, of the Swift County Historical Society, also provided generous assistance by supplying data on which this section is based.

difficulties in securing pastoral leadership. Church attendance was falling as young people left for the Twin Cities and elsewhere, though they often nostalgically kept their membership in the Lake Hazel Church.

In its most prosperous days, Lake Hazel was part of a network of rural Lutheran churches known informally as Benson's rural Lutheran parish. At one time this included Immanuel Lutheran in the city, Six Mile Grove just south of Benson, and Swift Falls just northeast of Benson. But as early as 1946 this parish was divided and reorganized, leaving Immanuel Church in the city of Benson as a separate church, and leaving Lake Hazel, Six Mile Grove, and Swift Falls on their own.

During the years Lake Hazel Church flourished, it was able to secure full-time pastoral service. In the mid-twentieth century, interim and temporary pastoral leadership became the rule.

On the second Sunday in June, 1967, the congregation had a farewell picnic, and two weeks later, on June 25, 1967, its membership gathered for its last worship service. As of July 1, 1967, Lake Hazel Lutheran was officially disbanded. An editorial in the local newspaper at the time correctly interpreted its abandonment as one more hostage to the new nonlocal forces coming to dominate life in post-twentieth-century America:

> Another rural church in this area has closed its doors, the congregation disbanded. The name of the game is "progress," an unavoidable constant that cannot be avoided, even though its inexorable advance is fended-off for a time.

SMALL TOWN AND THE NATION

However, it is doubtful if the values being sacrificed to progress, the heritage drowning in its wake, will be replaced by anything half as worthwhile.[11]

THE MEDICAL INSTITUTIONS OF BENSON

In the primitive world, illness is often treated as a purely personal and sometimes negatively magical condition. Not infrequently the ill person is taboo and placed in a sort of quarantine, in isolation from everyone. At other times, illness is assimilated to family patterns and treated as a special condition of dependency or it is assimilated to religion and treated as a punishment for sin. In any case, the effect of medical institutions, whether or not they be part of family, religious, or specialized institutions, is to give some sort of socially sanctioned response to illness. Through all such developments, illness has tended to remain primarily an affair of the individual and the primary group.

The modern understanding of disease has radically altered the inclination to permit diseases to remain as a more or less exclusively private concern. The key figure in the treatment of disease became the scientifically trained doctor, educated in an accredited medical school and licensed by the state. If nothing else, the doctor who came to practice in a small community like Benson was a representative of the

Conflicting Styles of Socialization

great world outside. The need for public health measures and the prevention of disease and the provision for medical needs of the aged and the handicapped increasingly brought more comprehensive political units, the state and federal governments, into the local picture.

As the scientifically equipped hospital moved into central position among institutions for dealing with disease, the small community rarely found it possible to finance one out of local resources. Various forms of translocal assistance may be sought by the small community for its hospital program, in which case the active initiative of the local community may itself be a major component in the increasing role of translocal medical institutions on the local scene.

While various translocal medical institutions of the state, of private organizations, and of the federal government play a role locally, Benson's hospital program and the changes attendant upon its success may be taken to illustrate the way local initiative may actually increase the role of translocal institutions.

In 1912, the Swift County Hospital was built in Benson at a cost of $15,000. In time, it became antiquated. Sparked by the president of the local hospital auxiliary, Mrs. Russell Hanson of Benson, in 1949 the local hospital auxiliary women raised over $60,000 locally to furnish the new hospital and to qualify for federal construction funds. This dramatic illustration of the enterprise of a tiny community was reported in newspapers across the United States. Mrs. Hanson, as president of the ladies auxiliary that produced the fund-raising miracle, became a consultant to local auxiliaries throughout the United States and abroad. More-

134

over, Mrs. Hanson was called on by the University of Minnesota College of Medical Sciences School of Public Health Program in Hospital Administration to share her knowledge of auxiliaries and volunteer services for hospitals with the class of graduate students studying hospital administration.

In a historical summary published in booklet form at the time the new hospital opened its doors, J. C. Mc Gowan, then publisher of the *Monitor-News,* summarized:

> Never before in the history of the community has there been an organization whose work was so needed, whose results so startling, and whose community spirit so unsurpassed as the Swift County-Benson hospital auxiliary. Unmistakably, the most outstanding contribution of the auxiliary was raising a whopping $60,146.66 for equipping the hospital. Without it, the federal aid, which is expected to materialize soon, would never have been available. Federal aid is based on amount of money on hand. For every $1 donated to the hospital, another 45 cents will be added by the federal government if no hitches develop. Today, the auxiliary boasts 2,061 members . . . the largest auxiliary in Minnesota. When its officers were first elected June 11, 1949, no one knew, hoped for, or suspected the spirit and accomplishment the auxiliary would bring to this community.[12]

July of 1949 saw membership rolls register a total of 1,143 women, and the auxiliary held a simulated "cocktail party for the hospital," collecting over 500 large cans of fruit and vegetable juices for the pantry in the new hospital.

The auxiliary staged a birthday jubilee in August and sought to collect pennies from everyone in Benson propor-

Conflicting Styles of Socialization

tionate to their ages. This netted $155. With this, and additional money raised from coffee parties, 20 wool blankets and 100 pairs of pillowcases were purchased.

The "mile of pennies" campaign was promoted, and September was designated as "refrigerator month" for obtaining refrigerators for the new hospital. Also, 530 washcloths and 613 bars of soap were collected for the new hospital's stockroom.

Harvest month was the October theme, and 1,000 cans of fruit and vegetable preserves were stored for the new hospital. Another committee went to work on a full set of draperies for the new hospital. Some 398 fine huck, dish, and bath towels were contributed for the new hospital's linen supply room in November, and individual donations of money began to increase.

A holiday party was held in December on behalf of the cause, and people flocked in with blankets, shirts, safety pins, and diapers as personal gifts to the proposed new "community of care, the hospital." Included were armloads of baby clothes for the pediatrics ward. Personal gifts totaled $1,000 for December alone.

A blood-donor program was led by Mrs. Alan Christensen, for the Red Cross blood bank, resulting in 710 donors and the beginning of a blood bank that would assure every Swift County resident an emergency supply of free blood.

In January and February, the auxiliary signed up 12,000 Swift County residents for chest X rays. A sewing committee cut and sewed 196 pillowcases, 96 sheets, and 15 pink pinafore uniforms for nurses' aids. At Benson's annual Kid Day, the "Kid Day Cops" managed to secure $50 in fines for the hospital's new baby bassinet.

Thirty-four girls volunteered as "hospital helpers" to read to patients, write letters for them, and generally both serve the hospital with informal help and explore for themselves future careers in nursing.

Auxiliary members saved coupons and redeemed them for the hospital fund. An exhibition baseball game was arranged between two rivals, the Benson Chiefs and the DeGraff Irish, and all proceeds, including umpires who paid their way in, went to the new hospital. And the Benson ball park was sold out with a capacity audience of 3,000 fans hanging on every pitch; $4,000 was raised in one night.

Up and down the street, business and professional men in Benson were badgered by the ladies for personal donations, the amounts publicized in the willing press of Joe McGowan. Individuals contributed amounts ranging from a $5,000 gift in the Erik Ostby estate to many contributions of $1,000 and $500. The slogan adopted by the auxiliary was, "Dig Deeper, This Time It's For Ourselves."

The hard results were: $60,146.66 raised from the pockets of Bensonites for Benson's new county-city hospital. Without this amount, the federal funds would not have been available to the extent that they were.

Benson's victorious auxiliary sent delegates to the Upper Midwest Hospital Conference, May 17, 1949, in Minneapolis, and a Benson woman was elected vice-president of the Minnesota auxiliary. The auxiliary itself was no longer only a locally autonomous structure, but became identified with the Minnesota State Hospital Auxiliaries Association and the American Hospital Association section on auxiliaries. And what had begun in Benson with a group of enthusiastic

Conflicting Styles of Socialization

women setting out to replace an antiquated hospital ended with the erection of a new forty-bed hospital in Benson, with that hospital's subsequent accreditation by the American College of Surgeons and the American Hospital Association.

In its legal title as a county-city hospital, there is evidence of a cleavage between local and nonlocal forces, as one-third of its budget is paid by county taxes and two-thirds by city taxes. Even the appointment of persons to its board of trustees reveals the tension between localism and nonlocalism: a specified proportion comes from the city of Benson itself and is appointed by the city council, while another proportion comes from the countywide jurisdiction of Swift County and is appointed by the Swift County board of county commissioners, who come from all over Swift County.

In the specialized staffing of the hospital, nonlocals are represented: a pathologist, who resides in nearby Litchfield, Minnesota, is on the staff. In addition, associate members of the Benson hospital medical staff include specialists from Willmar, Minnesota, and the Twin Cities. Three radiologists come from nearby Willmar to practice their medical specialty at the Benson hospital.

Furthermore, the American College of Surgeons and the American Hospital Association are national organizations within which the Benson hospital holds membership as a member hospital. Inasmuch as many small-town hospitals are unable to meet the standards of the American College of Surgeons and the American Hospital Association, the trustees of the Benson hospital are justifiably proud of their full accreditation. The periodic renewal of this accreditation comes only after the hospital passes an "examination" conducted by a specialist sent in from the American Hospital Association to observe the hospital and evaluate its standards.

Benson has a disproportionately large number (five) of doctors for a town in its population category, and in this respect is far more fortunate than many small towns that are without doctors. Of Benson's five M.D.'s, one practices as a solo practitioner, and the others form two different practices with two members each. Of Swift County's seven practicing doctors, Benson has five (nearby Appleton claims the other two). One of the reasons cited for Benson's ability to claim five practicing doctors is its forty-bed hospital facility.

ANALYTICAL SURVEY OF SOCIALIZATION

Socialization Characteristics

The same samples of old- and new-style Bensonites utilized to explore the patterns of economic characteristics and economic attitudes were also employed in the investigation of the characteristics and attitudes in the sphere of socialization. The responses to the items were coded in such a manner that the traits reflecting localism would receive lower scores. If the groups systematically differed in the predicted manner, the mean score of old-style Bensonites would be lower than the mean score of new-style Bensonites. For example, it was possible that the new-style Bensonites as a group would be younger, possess more education, be less religious, be less often married, less often have parents born in Benson, and less often belong to the dominant nationalities of Benson. Systematic higher scores on all these points would indicate a tendency by new-style Bensonites to differ in all these respects. The findings are given in Table 39. Only one item failed to show the predicted pattern.

If one computed the total group mean it was possible to run chi-square tests on the significance of the difference of the distribution of the scores of the two groups around the group mean.

To some extent the general findings were strengthened by the fact that the two samples did not differ significantly with respect to age and parental origin. This means that other differences could not be attributed to an age differential or to a contrast between people with parents born in Benson and those born outside. In marital status the new-style Bensonites actually reversed expectation, though the difference was not significant.

TABLE 39

SOCIALIZATION CHARACTERISTICS OF BENSONITES

| | Mean Scores | | |
CHARACTERISTIC	Old-Style	New-Style	Predicted
Age	2.00	4.13	Yes
Education	4.31	4.78	Yes
Religion	6.05	6.51	Yes
Marital status	1.63	1.00	No
Nationality	3.36	5.37	Yes

TABLE 40

SIGNIFICANCE OF THE DIFFERENCES OF SOCIALIZATION
CHARACTERISTICS BETWEEN OLD- AND NEW-STYLE BENSONITES

CHARACTERISTIC	Chi-Squares	Significance[a]
Age	1.60	NS[b]
Education	3.49	.05
Religion	4.46	.05
Marital status	2.29	NS
Parental origin	1.58	NS
Nationality	7.23	.01

[a] At one degree of freedom.
[b] NS = not significant.

Socialization Attitudes of Old-
and New-Style Bensonites

A total of seventeen statements were presented to the sample groups to which they could respond positively or negatively. These were scored in such a manner that low scores would indicate localism; high scores, cosmopolitanism. It was anticipated that the scores of old-style Bensonites would be lower than those of new-style Bensonites.

The contrast between new- and old-style Bensonites in socialization attitudes is striking. On only two items did the means not fall in the anticipated direction. Those two items ("To be really educated one should study in Europe" and "There are good points to Benson that money cannot buy") could possibly have been answered more positively by Benson's cosmopolitans because of translocal properties of their outlook. In knowing more about the outside world, cosmopolitans may be less inclined to overestimate it. Furthermore, the cosmopolitans may with greater

TABLE 41

SOCIALIZATION ATTITUDES OF OLD- AND NEW-STYLE BENSONITES

STATEMENT	Mean Scores		
	Old-Style	New-Style	Predicted
The young lack respect for their elders	2.94	3.43	Yes
Education should adjust the young to Benson	3.78	5.21	Yes
One should teach Benson's history	2.94	3.48	Yes
Education should prepare the young for the outside world	6.15	6.24	Yes
In school, the young should read whatever they wish	2.84	3.05	Yes
Too few young people plan to remain in Benson	2.89	3.32	Yes
To be really educated one should study in Europe	2.61	2.5	No
Religion is essential to successful, happy life	1.84	1.96	Yes
There are Bensonites who think religion is not necessary	4.84	5.00	Yes
People should remain true to religion they were reared in	3.36	4.35	Yes
Interfaith marriages do not work	3.84	4.89	Yes
Marriages between social equals are best	2.94	3.16	Yes
The family should have a voice in marriage decisions	4.68	5.05	Yes
Marriages between divorced persons do not work	4.21	5.00	Yes
There are good points to Benson that money cannot buy	2.52	2.51	No
A small town is the best place to live	2.52	2.94	Yes
Life in a small town is more wholesome than in a big city	2.10	2.18	Yes

SMALL TOWN AND THE NATION

TABLE 42

SIGNIFICANCE OF THE DIFFERENCES OF SOCIALIZATION ATTITUDES BETWEEN OLD- AND NEW-STYLE BENSONITES

STATEMENT	Chi-Squares	Significance[a]
The young lack respect for their elders	1.24	NS[b]
Education should adjust the young to Benson	1.18	NS
One should teach Benson's history	2.36	NS
Education should prepare the young for the outside world	2.00	NS
In school, the young should read whatever they wish	5.09	.05
Too few young people plan to remain in Benson	8.91	.01
To be really educated one should study in Europe	1.46	NS
Religion is essential to successful, happy life	1.46	NS
There are Bensonites who think religion is not necessary	1.11	NS
People should remain true to the religion they were reared in	7.12	.01
Interfaith marriages do not work	1.12	NS
Marriages between social equals are best	1.13	NS
The family should have a voice in marriage decisions	5.56	.02
Marriages between divorced persons do not work	8.46	.01
There are good points to Benson that money cannot buy	5.18	.05
A small town is the best place to live	5.09	.05
Life in a small town is more wholesome than in a big city	1.80	NS

[a] At one degree of freedom.
[b] NS = not significant.

143

Conflicting Styles of Socialization

frequency have made the self-conscious decision to stay in Benson despite opportunities elsewhere and hence are more inclined to stress its uniqueness.

While only seven of the attitude contrasts were statistically significant and while one of these was in the wrong direction, the systematic difference in attitude between old and new style is beyond any question.

Bensonites and the Control Group of Ex-Bensonites

When old-style Bensonites were compared with a control group of ex-Bensonites, systematic differences in socialization characteristics and attitudes tended to appear, comparable to those between the two experimental groups. When new-style Bensonites were compared with the control group, the two groups were found to be very similar. Since there is no particular value in detailed discussions of the various contrasts between experimental groups and the samples, the data are not included in the text. The various sample means and chi-square differences do appear in the appendix.

SOME SUMMARY OBSERVATIONS

In the present study we did not examine the extent to which the family and such basic socialization institutions as child-rearing practices in Benson reflect the influence of

144

translocal forces and trends. We did inquire into some features of Benson's education, religion, and health institutions. Our analytical survey of samples of old- and new-style Bensonites did not include items on health and welfare, but did include characteristics and items on the family, education, and religion.

While Benson's education remains primarily a local affair governed and paid for out of local resources, many translocal forces and trends are evident. For one thing, the rural schools are closing down and their students are now bussed into the consolidated schools of the nearby small towns. Ironically Benson's city schools are playing the role of translocal educational institution to the countryside. The autonomy of the remaining twelve ungraded rural schools is near an end.

Benson, like other small towns, must obtain teachers trained outside the area. They bring translocal perspectives with them. The curriculum must meet standards that permit graduates to compete with the graduates of the big city schools or their graduates will be crippled in the competition. In the course of such developments, the costs of education increase beyond local resources and the small schools must seek state or federal aid.

There is, thus, in the educational institutions a spiral of involvement with the translocal scene and its cultural peculiarities.

Though Bensonites, like most other Americans, strenuously resist outside interference with their religious institutions, their religion, too, displays a response to translocal trends. The consolidated church is replacing the isolated rural church. The role of the pastor is slowly acquiring features that make him look more like a service-oriented social worker than the old-time saver of souls. The content of the religious message shows less preoccupation with sin, damnation, and salvation and a growing preoccupation with social problems. Congregations are beginning to erode somewhat in a manner suggestive of big-city influence and movements toward affiliation with translocal organizations are underway.

In the field of health and medicine, translocal influence is again present in many forms and degrees. The health department of the state is somewhere in the background in problems of public health and in some areas of preventive medicine. The federal government has come directly into the citizens' daily lives with Medicare. The doctors and physicians and dentists are trained in translocal institutions and meet the standards of their professional organizations and state licensing bodies.

The hospital has moved to the center of the medical practice. But the costs of a scientifically equipped and staffed hospital often exceed the resources of the local community. The Benson hospital drive illustrates the manner in which heroic local effort was directed to qualifying for federal assistance, and reveals the many-faceted involvement with other translocal institutions that came with the hospital.

It is not surprising, in view of all these evidences of the presence of local and translocal forces in Benson's institutions of socialization, that sharp differences should be found between old- and new-style Bensonites both in socialization characteristics and attitudes. Two distinct philosophies of socialization appear between the groups.

146

1. "Philosophy of the Benson Public Schools," Descriptive Material for Faculty Members, mimeographed (Benson, Minn.: Public Schools, n.d.), p. 4.

2. *Ibid.*

3. *Ibid.*

4. *Ibid.*

5. *Ibid.*

6. *Ibid.,* p. 5.

7. *Swift County* (Minn.) *Monitor,* June 8, 1967, sec. 2, p. 1.

8. *Swift County* (Minn.) *News,* October 11, 1967, p. 1.

9. *Swift County* (Minn.) *Monitor,* June 8, 1967, p. 1.

10. *Light and Life* (Benson, Minn.: Our Redeemer's Lutheran Church, June, 1967), p. 2.

11. *Swift County* (Minn.) *Monitor,* July 6, 1967, p. 4.

12. *Yearbook 1949–1950* of Swift County–Benson Hospital Auxiliary (Benson, Minn.: privately printed, 1949), p. 30.

8

THE CONFRONTATIONS OF POWER AND INFLUENCE

S ocial control consists of the manner in which the interests of the individual and those of society are combined
and ordered.[1] A variety of municipal institutions integrate
the individual interests of Bensonites with the collective
interest. The Jeffersonian ideal of keeping the role of government minimal is still strong in Benson. The enactments
of Benson's city council concern such matters as the conditions
under which liquor is sold in the municipal liquor store, the

rules for the licensing of dogs or bicycles, disturbances of the peace, civic traffic offenses, and property. Since Bensonites also live in the governmental unit of Swift County (the courthouse is located in Benson), it, too, exercises control over many of their activities. The Swift County sheriff enforces laws and serves legal papers as directed by the appropriate courts. Officials of the state and federal governments occasionally appear in Benson to deal with matters in their respective jurisdictions. Bensonites are called to jury duty on cases involving their fellow citizens. They participate in political parties, in pressure groups, and in service organizations. Bensonites are represented in the state legislature by a state representative and a state senator. They are represented in the United States House of Representatives in Washington, D.C. In short, a wide variety of agencies and institutions of social control are operating in Benson.

BENSON MUNICIPAL GOVERNMENT

The old courthouse, which houses the county government, is one center of control, but municipal government in Benson is centered on the other side of the railroad tracks in the Municipal Building.

Like an enlarged crackerbox with neatly fitting compartments providing space for city clerk, council chambers, and the city jail and cell block, the Municipal Building is

The Confrontations of Power and Influence

the nerve center of Benson government. In buildings on different sides of it are housed the city light plant and the city fire department.

The municipal offices of Benson include those of the mayor, the city manager, city council, city attorney, city clerk, and chief of police. Other major city organizations include the city fire department, the city disposal plant, the city light plant, municipal liquor store, the Benson public library, the street maintenance section, water and light maintenance, and the section on city parks and playgrounds.

The "Great Debate": Should Civic Office be Salaried?

As of early August, 1967, Benson, Sauk Centre, and Tracy were the only Minnesota towns of their size that did not pay salaries to the mayor and the members of the city council.[2] The issue was hotly contested, and twice in the recent past in special elections Bensonites defeated the proposal to pay the mayor and council. At the time, salaries could only be instituted by popular vote. However, in 1967, the Minnesota state legislature passed a law that placed the question in the exclusive hands of the council, which was empowered to set up a salary for its members after the 1968 municipal elections.

With passage of this law, the issue came before the council. On Wednesday, August 9, 1967, a prominent Benson businessman and civic leader, Robert Hawley, stated his opposition to unilateral action by the council in setting up their own salary, arguing that the decision should be left in the hands of the voters since the state legislature did not make the new law mandatory on city governing bodies. Hawley further argued that though the initial figure for the salaries for mayor and council was low, its adoption could open the door for greater increases in the future. Finally, contended Hawley, city government is one of the few remaining forms of government where people may serve purely as voluntary public servants.[3] The city council judiciously noted Hawley's contentions one by one, but approved their wage plan.

> An ordinance establishing salaries for the mayor and council has been passed by the council. Under the new law, the mayor would receive $50 per month and councilmen $35 per month, starting after the next municipal election. If either the mayor or a council member is absent from a meeting, without excuse, they will be fined $10 upon majority vote of councilmen present. At present, Benson, Tracy, and Sauk Centre are the only known municipalities of from 1,000 to 5,000 population not paying salaries to their council and mayor.[4]

Localism and Translocalism in the "Great Debate"

The law passed by the Minnesota state legislature, which allowed the Benson city council to bypass the local voters in adopting their wage plan, demonstrates the impact of translocal forces on local social control. The public justification for adoption of the wage plan was "to align Benson with the rest of the state,"[5] also illustrating the clash between translocalism and localism. Even after the council's final approval of the wage plan, discussion raged among Bensonites. Those supporting the council action argued that

151

it was about time Benson got in the swim with the rest of the towns of its size in managing municipal affairs; those opposing the council action typically countered, "So what? The issue is not the other towns in Minnesota, but what we decide to do on our own in Benson."

Police Protection for Benson

The chief of police and the police force in Benson are employees of the city, with the chief hired by the council. The council also takes sealed bids from automobile dealers and takes action to purchase the police car. Traffic offenders are arrested, the safety of Benson's streets is maintained, regular rounds are made to maintain surveillance of property, and accidents are investigated.

Police headquarters and a cell block are located in the Municipal Building. A community of Benson's size normally requires only one police station.[6] Careless motorists who run afoul of the Benson police make the acquaintance of another of Benson's institutions for social control, the justice of peace court.

Benson's Justice of the Peace Court

While many communities have replaced their traditional justice of the peace courts with new municipal courts for the handling of petty offenses on the local scene, Benson remains traditionalistic. Traffic violations, disturbances of the peace, writing bad checks are among the types of charges that might appear before the local justice of the peace court.

152

And at intervals, the Benson newspaper publishes a column with the names of those who have appeared before the court and the charges against them.

The justice of the peace is a last vestige of the frontier social control system in contemporary America, maintaining a high degree of autonomy in the way justice is determined, often running his court with little or no legal training. There is no unified national system of justices of the peace which compares to, say, the district courts. The exact number of justice of the peace courts in the nation is unknown. In the view of the national court system, they have the tendency to become kangaroo courts. This is not to question the quality of justice of the justice of the peace courts in general nor of the justice of the peace court in Benson in particular, but to call attention to their character as local institutions of control.

Translocal forces are undercutting the autonomy of the local justice of the peace, for cases before him may indeed be appealed to a court with wider jurisdiction and less local autonomy. Furthermore, the unmistakable trend is toward the development of municipal courts in place of the justice of the peace courts.

Parking Meters in Benson

An interesting example of the displacement of old local patterns by procedures typical of the larger urban complexes is presented by the advent of parking meters. The Benson city government maintains parking meters on the two main streets in the downtown business area. The purpose is twofold: to exercise some control over spaces that used to be taken up indiscriminately; and to gain additional revenue for the city. Income from the meters runs around $7,000 a year, with $1,600 paid out for their yearly upkeep.[7]

Since their installation, the parking meters have been a bone of contention among Bensonites. The general breakdown of opinion has pitted older style Bensonites against the meters, and the younger in their favor. Another source of complaints has been the farmers, who believe their patronage is vital to Benson's prosperity and do not interpret the parking meters as a welcome mat. Those in favor of the meters cite the need to control motor vehicle parking, the need for more revenue, and the desirability of making Benson appear less like a village. Those against the meters see them as one more inroad into the old autonomy of the town.

The Fire Department

Benson's progressive fire department is composed of local men who are willing to give their time and also incur possible personal risk in order to protect Benson from fire. They are a perfect example of what Benson businessman Robert Hawley referred to as the characteristic of city government offering opportunity for service on a purely volunteer basis.

These volunteers conduct bingo to raise money for their fire hall and maintenance of its equipment. They maintain a well-organized strategy for dealing with emergencies. They participate with departments across the state in certain public education campaigns. For example, when fire departments all over Minnesota conducted a public education campaign, Preparation Edith, to educate the public about fire dangers

154

in the home, the local force joined in.[8] In emergencies, fire departments from neighboring towns extend help to one another.

COUNTY GOVERNMENT

Benson is a county seat town. Offices and jurisdictions centered in the Swift County courthouse are: the county attorney, the county auditor, the county clerk of court, the county coroner, the county engineer, the extension service, the county garage system, the county health officer, the county historical society, the judge of probate, the county nurse's office, the county register of deeds, the county sheriff, the county superintendent of schools, the county supervisor of assessments, the county treasurer, the veterans' service officer, and county welfare officials. There is a courtroom in the courthouse, and a judge of the district court travels into Benson from another city to preside over court here.

In the more urbanized areas of Minnesota, there are special juvenile courts to deal with the adjudication of juveniles. But in Benson, and in Swift County, this is dealt with through the office of the judge of probate, whose office is in the courthouse.

This proliferation of role in county government in Benson is typical in other areas as well. For example, in addition to matters of court record and procedure, the clerk of court handles applications for drivers' licenses in the Swift County area for the state of Minnesota and other matters also.

The Swift County sheriff engages in law enforcement from his offices in the courthouse, and his role covers a far-ranging series of tasks, from investigation of reported criminalities and violations to the serving of legal papers for the court. The county sheriff and the Benson city police cooperate with one another. Similarly, the Swift County sheriff cooperates with law-enforcement officers in other adjacent counties and municipalities as well. Many problems are translocal in nature and are dealt with by local city and county law officers in cooperation with translocal law-enforcement officers.

County commissioners are elected to serve on the Swift County board, and this group of elected officials pass on budgeting matters for the maintenance of county roads, on county welfare, county law enforcement, and other jurisdictional issues. They are elected on an area basis, thus assuring representation on the board from the geographical whole of the county.

But there is constant awareness that the importance of county government is declining. As the number of rural ungraded schools continues to diminish, for example, the need for the office of county superintendent of schools also diminishes. There is increased discussion of the possibility that autonomous and duplicative procedures of rural, scattered counties be consolidated. Otto Herfindahl, a seasoned Swift County politician-farmer who, before his death, served for a time as an elected county commissioner, observed: "Rural counties are going to find it harder to stay above water, as more and more of the people and the resources are held by the bigger cities."

THE FEDERAL GOVERNMENT
IN BENSON

The municipal government in Benson deals primarily with minor offenses such as licenses for dogs, bicycles, liquor sold at the municipal store, and the like. The range of matters dealt with by the county government is generally more important. However, the sphere of county government is also being curtailed. Correspondingly, the sphere of state and federal government is expanding, moving into the spaces that local government once occupied and from which it is gradually being evicted. At the same time, state and federal government enactments proceed from the requirements of these larger wholes.

As the farmers do more and more of their business directly with the federal government it is increasingly convenient for various federal agencies to establish branch offices in various localities they serve. The following branch offices of the federal government are maintained in Benson: the Department of Agricultural Stabilization and Conservation Commission; the national armory in Benson, which houses the national guard installation; the Farmers Home Administration; the Federal Crop Insurance Office; the U.S. Fish and Wildlife Service; the Neighborhood Youth Corps program installation; the Minnesota division of the Federal Forestry Service; the local board of the Selective Service; the Soil and Conservation Office; and the U.S. Post Office in Benson.

This important complex of federal government offices does considerable business directly with Benson citizens and enforces a variety of federal laws and regulations.

TRANSLOCAL ASPECTS OF THE POLITICAL PARTIES

Both the Republican and the Democratic Farmer-Labor parties are organized in Benson on the local level. A Swift County convention is held by the respective parties for election of a slate of officers and delegates to translocal conventions. The chosen delegates from the Benson area then travel to the site of the Sixth Congressional District conventions, and, at four-year intervals, some persons from the Benson area will probably be chosen by their party colleagues to be delegates to the national conventions that choose Presidential nominees and write national political platforms. Benson's grass-roots politics is linked to state and national politics. Bensonites still remember a local Lutheran clergyman who in the early years of this century announced to his astonished parishioners from his pulpit one Sunday morning that he was running for the United States Congress. That

Benson clergyman, O. J. Kvale, went on to serve in the Congress and had a brilliant career as a progressive, independent influence in Benson's congressional district and the nation.

However, the movement is by no means only from the local to the translocal scene. Figures from campaign expenses in the 1966 campaign in Benson's congressional district reveal that the winner, John Zwach, received $10,000 from *national* Republican organizations with which to finance his campaign throughout the Sixth Congressional District.[9] Thus, in the political parties, local and translocal forces meet.

AGENCIES OF INFLUENCE: THE PRESS

In the theory of social control a distinction is sometimes made between the institutions of power, such as the state, the police, and the courts, which possess coercive sanctions, and the agencies of influence, such as the press and social strata, which exercise influence over events but only possess informal noncoercive sanctions.

If pressed to a choice between either a newspaper or a government, Thomas Jefferson once confessed that he would take the newspaper. In Benson today, the local newspaper and radio station exert vital roles in shaping collective inter-

The Confrontations of Power and Influence

ests. Local and translocal forces are at work on Benson's press.

Broadcast Media: KBMO Radio

This station is locally owned and its staff people reside for the most part in Benson. However, much of its news comes in translocally via the United Press International wire. Moreover, local dealers who advertise on local radio may be aided in the payment of their advertising by the national or regional office of the product for which they hold a local franchise.

Without its press-wire hookup with a teletype from the wider world, KBMO would have to read its world news from a newspaper like any subscriber. Furthermore, the translocal process is demonstrated by advertisers from outside Benson's city limits who find it, nevertheless, advantageous to use KBMO's airways to sell their products or services. And KBMO maintains studios in nearby Appleton, another indication of translocal ties. Finally, KBMO is on the air only because it has been able to secure and renew its license from the federal government (the Federal Communications Commission) to serve the public interest, necessity, and convenience as a broadcasting station.

The Local Newspaper in Benson

The old *Swift County Democrat* was purchased by T. F. Young, Ed Young, and D. Y. Smith, who decided to rename the paper the *Monitor*. Their first issue appeared in 1886. Since then the ownership has changed from time to time, but the publication record is unbroken. As a taste-

160

setter, summarizer, reporter, editorialist, humorist, carrier of advertisements and local society news, it has an unequaled record in providing Bensonites with news, information, and entertainment. An examination of the issues of both the *Monitor* and the *News* from August, 1966, through August, 1967, provides ample evidence of the dramatic confrontation in Benson today between local and translocal forces.

For example, the August 25, 1966, issue reveals the results of an economic survey which found that 20 percent of the Bensonites interviewed buy clothes and shoes *outside* Benson.[11] J. L. Edman, the county agent for Swift County, writes a column called "Farm News 'n Views" in the *Monitor* which brings to mind that it was federal legislation that enabled rural American counties to reap the great benefits of the county agent system.[10]

Its background was closely interwoven with the history of the land-grant-college and grants-in-aid systems.

The land-grant-college system was established in 1862 by the Morrill Act, which granted to each loyal state 30,000 acres—apportioned for each of its senators and representatives in Congress—in order to found and endow much-needed agricultural colleges. Under its provisions the sixty-nine land-grant colleges serve as centers for study and research in the agricultural sciences, and bring new knowledge and techniques to the American farmer. Thus the land-grant college is a liaison between the national government and the rural citizen.

Through the cooperation of the Department of Agriculture and the land-grant colleges, the Smith-Lever Act, in 1914, provided a system for further agricultural education extension centers, and provided that federal grants-in-aid be matched by state appropriations. It established a country-wide system of county agents who served as liaison between the agricultural colleges, their extension stations, and the farmer.

The local county agent, writing a popular column in the local newspaper, brings the problems and ideas of the national government into the local milieu; he thus provides another vital link between the purpose and organization of state and national governments and the local citizen.

There is a wealth of wild ducks and pheasants in Benson's countryside. Benson's *Swift County Monitor,* in its September 6, 1966 issue, carried two articles reporting on non-local efforts to develop and capitalize on these natural resources. One of these articles was a report on the pheasant brood, released by Minnesota's Game and Fish Director, the other discussed the modification of the duckling release program sponsored by the state's Future Farmers of America. In both cases, local conservation efforts were supplemented by translocal efforts.[12] Teachers coming from outside areas to begin their teaching duties in Benson schools were pictured in the September 6 issue of the paper.[13]

The article on the primary election reported news of elective contests on both the local and state levels.[14]

The October 27, 1966, *Monitor* reported the dedication of the new Benson post office building scheduled for the upcoming Sabbath at which Congressman Alec Olson of the U.S. House of Representatives was to be present, as would Clifford R. Mitchell, postal service officer representing the U.S. Post Office Department.[15]

Announcement of a $475,000 loan from the Rural Electrification Association to Agralite of Benson was made in

SMALL TOWN AND THE NATION

the newspaper, and a detailed enumeration given of the way the money would be spent locally. Federal funds were loaned for local use, and again the dramatic encounter between local and translocal forces was reflected in the reportage of the local newspaper.[16]

When the local area branch of the National Farmers' Organization dumped 50,000 pounds of milk into the ditch to demonstrate their dissatisfaction with prices paid to dairy farmers, the *Monitor* gave the story the headline it deserved. Here were local farmers joining hands to dump milk rather than sell it for inequitable prices. Moreover, the local farmers were joined in a *national* withholding action, and this is another graphic example of the local meeting the national in Benson's immediate life.[17]

On June 8, 1967, the *Monitor* reported the number of Swift County persons on Social Security, a striking reminder of the role of translocalism in Benson's survival.[18]

The local newspaper not only documents the presence of local and translocal forces in Benson's community life, but is itself oriented to both types of forces.

THE ANALYTICAL SURVEY OF SOCIAL CONTROL IN BENSON

Control Characteristics

The samples of old- and new-style Bensonites were examined for differential characteristics and attitudes in the sphere of

The Confrontations of Power and Influence

social control. Among the properties it was theorized would indicate an individual's comparative power and influence were such things as political preference, the number of organizational affiliations, the number of local positions, the number of translocal positions held, the number of friends active in Benson political parties, the number of friends in Benson city government, and the number of community influentials with whom one shares house visits. As in the case of other properties on which the sample was examined, it was assumed that old-style Bensonites were oriented inward to the local scene and new-style Bensonites were oriented toward translocal forces in the community and toward the world outside. The responses were scored in such a manner that low scores would be indicative of localism, high scores

TABLE 43

DIFFERENCES ON SELECTED SOCIAL CONTROL CHARACTERISTICS BETWEEN OLD- AND NEW-STYLE BENSONITES

| CHARACTERISTIC | Mean Scores | | Predicted |
	Old-Style	New-Style	
Political preference	3.68	2.94	No
Number of organizational affiliations	3.10	3.27	Yes
Local positions held	1.94	1.91	No
Translocal positions held	1.52	1.21	No
Friends active in Benson politics	3.36	3.91	Yes
Friends in Benson government	3.21	3.64	Yes
Table community with influentials	5.07	5.32	Yes

TABLE 44

SCORE DISTRIBUTIONS ON CONTROL CHARACTERISTICS
OF OLD- AND NEW-STYLE BENSONITES

CHARACTERISTIC	Chi-Squares	Significance[a]
Political preference	7.34	.01
Number of organizational affiliations	8.40	.01
Local positions held	2.83	NS[b]
Translocal positions held	2.73	NS
Friends active in Benson politics	7.07	.01
Friends in Benson city government	2.83	NS
Table community with influentials	1.64	NS

[a] At one degree of freedom.
[b] NS = not significant.

of cosmopolitanism. If the scoring was correct and the samples differed in the ways theorized, the mean scores of the two groups should reveal this (Table 43).

Four out of seven of the characteristics examined were as predicted. The significance of the differences is also relevant (Table 44).

While only three of the items were significant at the .01 level, three others approached significance. If one takes together the distribution of means and the items on which the difference was or approached statistical significance, it would appear that in social control characteristics the old- and new-style Bensonites are, in fact, quite different.

Attitude Differences of the Sample Groups

A number of statements were posed for the sample groups having to do with local and translocal social control matters.

TABLE 45

SOCIAL-CONTROL ATTITUDES OF
OLD- AND NEW-STYLE BENSONITES

| | Mean Scores | | |
STATEMENT	*Old-Style*	*New-Style*	Predicted
Small towns should get money for rural renewal	3.21	3.64	Yes
The federal government should stay out of local politics	5.07	5.32	Yes
Political power should remain at local level	2.84	3.05	Yes
Reapportionment was right in taking power away from rural areas	2.89	3.32	Yes
Government is best that does the least	2.63	2.51	No
Farmers should have collective bargaining	1.84	1.86	Yes
The NFO is doing a real service	4.84	5.00	Yes
Civic groups should try to get more industry into Benson	3.84	4.89	Yes
Only by voting can one influence local government	2.94	3.16	Yes
Local politics in Benson is too complicated	4.68	5.05	Yes
Parking meters are good for Benson	4.21	5.00	Yes
Local Benson politicians are indifferent	3.15	4.13	Yes
Benson's old families still have power	2.47	2.62	Yes
Benson's newcomers get things done	1.73	1.81	Yes

It was theorized that old-style Bensonites would respond with more sympathy to matters enhancing local controls than would new-style Bensonites. The response categories were

TABLE 46

SCORE DISTRIBUTIONS ON ATTITUDE ITEMS BY OLD- AND NEW-STYLE BENSONITES

STATEMENT	Chi-Squares	Significance[a]
Small town should get money for rural renewal	1.33	NS[b]
The federal government should stay out of local politics	1.60	NS
Political power should remain at local level	2.39	NS
Reapportionment was right in taking power away from rural areas	2.94	NS
Government is best that does the least	1.27	NS
Farmers should have collective bargaining	4.22	.05
The NFO is doing a real service	6.48	.02
Civic groups should try to get more industry into Benson	4.91	.05
Only by voting can one influence local government	7.05	.01
Local politics in Benson is too complicated	7.75	.01
Parking meters are good for Benson	1.31	NS
Local Benson politicians are indifferent	7.38	.01
Benson's old families still have power	6.75	.01
Benson's newcomers get things done	1.07	NS

[a] At one degree of freedom.
[b] NS = not significant.

scored in a manner giving lower scores for localism, higher scores for cosmopolitanism. Again the prediction was that on any given attitude item, old-style Bensonites would present a lower mean score than new-style Bensonites. On all but one out of fourteen items the difference was as predicted.

When the two samples were combined and a group mean was found on each item, it was possible to calculate

The Confrontations of Power and Influence

Chi-squares on the distribution of sample scores around the group mean. On approximately half of the items, the chi-squares were significant at the .05 or higher level. In a few other instances, the differences approached significance.

When the two sets of findings are taken together there is no question that systematic differences in attitudes on social control appear between old- and new-style Bensonites.

Bensonites and Ex-Bensonites

As in the case of attitudes in the spheres of economics and socialization, ex-Bensonites were close to the new-style Bensonites and systematically more cosmopolitan than old-style Bensonites. Data for checking the specific differences appear in the appendix.

OVERVIEW OF SOCIAL CONTROL IN BENSON

City, county, state, and federal political, police, and judicial institutions operate in Benson. The role of the city and county in social control grows ever smaller; that of the state and federal governments grows ever larger. The way the state may directly transform civic politics was illustrated by the enactment of the Minnesota law giving city councils exclusive decision-making in setting their own salaries. Benson's citizens, who had twice rejected such a proposal when it had to be voted on, now had no elective choice in the matter.

The county courthouse with halls that echo like a museum containing artifacts from the past carries on its routine of registering deeds in its giant record ledgers, recording birth certificates, collecting taxes, making audits, supervising a few rural schools, processing probate and other legal matters. However, there is a strong possibility that soon it, along with other counties, will be forced to combine into rural regions and consolidated counties.

The role of the federal government on the local scene is increasing, with branches of the federal forestry, wildlife, and soil conservation divisions taking an active part in Benson's life. The farmers conduct business directly with the federal government, circumventing all intermediate structures.

Agencies of influence such as the press have ties with national networks and press wires, again revealing the presence of local and translocal forces.

With all this evidence of the intersection of local and translocal institutions or agencies of social control, it would logically follow that individuals caught in the crossfire would incline toward one or the other set of forces. The analytical survey indicated that at least with respect to political preferences, number of organizational affiliations, and friends active in local politics, there were significant differences between old- and new-style Bensonites. When the political attitudes toward local and translocal matters of these two groups were measured, often slight but systematic contrasts appeared. The two groups were bearers of distinct ways of life.

169

If we accept the fact that the analytical survey established beyond any doubt the presence in Benson of two distinct ways of life, it is possible to interpret somewhat more fully two political issues that were generating considerable local heat at the time of the study. These issues were the payment of city officials and parking meters.

For Benson's entire history until the recent council enactment, the offices of mayor and councilmen were unpaid. The compensation of office holders was a matter of personal satisfaction and the esteem of their neighbors. They were a type of officialdom described by Max Weber in his famous essay "Politics as a Vocation." Weber described a political administration of persons who serve without pay as a government by notables and individuals who serve under such circumstances as living "for" rather than "off" politics.[19]

In the nature of the case, as long as political office is an unpaid duty it will be accepted only by those who can afford it. Power will tend, under such circumstances, to reside in the hands of one or a few families, and the real decisions binding on the community are often made by influentials of this circle at private gatherings. In his study of power in Regional City, Floyd Hunter observes: "The men in Regional City who hold power gather strength in many instances from association with their fellows on an informal and light-hearted level. . . . The luncheon clubs provide a good place in which to exchange ideas, thus helping keep a kind of like-mindedness."[20]

This was decidedly the case in Benson in the last generation before the present when power was in the hands of old-style Bensonites, among whom representatives of a num-

SMALL TOWN AND THE NATION

ber of eminent families served in public office largely without compensation. Key persons from these strata routinely met winter and summer on a daily basis for ten o'clock coffee and in season for golf at five in the afternoon. They came to be known as the Ten O'clock Club, and it was said that no decision was made without their consent.

Members of this informal clique were on Benson's Main Street: owners of town businesses, a few important professionals, and a few local entrepreneurs and financiers. No significant local happening escaped the grapevine that fed information to its members. In some instances, it was reported to the researchers, on fast-breaking matters they gathered on the spur of the moment to decide the course of action, which in most instances became binding on the community. The notables who ruled Benson in the past did so at their own expense and saw politics as a public service. They ran the town in their own interest and were not expected to do otherwise. Yet their own interest was mediated with an enlightened concern for the interests of others. For they could maintain their prestige only so long as they acted with responsibility toward the town as a whole.

The dynastic families of Old Benson had several prototypical models: prominent mercantile, professional, financial, and agricultural families. They were expected to deport themselves with a style that is disappearing. As one grand dame of the old-style tradition put it: "They [the new wielders of power] walk around this town as if they think one family is just like any other, and their ignorance is proven by their brashness."

Thus, the issue over the payment or nonpayment of

171

---

mayor and council reflects the rise of a new type of power-holder cultivating a new style: the paid politician, in Weber's terms, who made a living from his political activities and lived "off" politics. The objective of the professional politician is to stay in power, not to use his office to sustain some special system of social relations.

The new-style leader in Benson is typified by the city manager, the chamber of commerce manager, the new salaried mayorship, and the new salaried cabinet-council. They understand their task as one of turning their backs on the past and bringing the community into the twentieth century. Political service is something to be bought and paid for like any other service, and the purchaser (the general public) has a right to the service it pays for and must not be in a position of receiving political service on a charity basis.

The style of the new wielder of power is more impersonal even when it is more responsive to the electorate at large rather than to the local high status groups.

Members of the new power clique see the old guard as conservative, unresponsive to contemporary trends, and rather anachronistic. Members of the old families that supplied the old-style government with officials see the new wielders of power as hirelings. As the grand old lady of the old order put it: "The new politicians in Benson are mere, minor paid functionaries. . . . Whereas our pay, when my husband was alive, our pay was our respect."

This changing style of power and influence which has tended to shift from old-style to new-style Bensonites provides the major reason for the conflict over parking meters. Since all groups admit that parking meters bring needed

172

revenue to the town it would be a mystery why there should be any conflict at all if one did not take into account the symbolic significance of the meters.

In Old Benson, one could stop one's car in the middle of the street while one exchanged civilities with a neighbor. The street operated like a general all-purpose meeting place where the ladies stopped to chat, where children shouted greetings to one another, where boys gathered with their bicycles to plan a raid on one of the nearby apple orchards, and where young men and women made a date. The street symbolized the sociability and sharing of a self-oriented community.

In New Benson, the street is being converted into an efficient thoroughfare and municipal parking area calculated to speed individuals on their business or to return a small fine for overparking into the public treasury. To the new-style Bensonite the stalling, traffic-blocking proclivities of the old-timers are "dog-patchy" examples of rural nostalgia. They wish to give their town the look of streamlined efficiency of the metropolis.

NOTES

1. Don Martindale, *The Nature and Types of Sociological Theory* (Boston: Houghton Mifflin Co., 1960), p. 322.

2. *Swift County* (Minn.) *Monitor,* August 10, 1967, p. 1.

3. *Ibid.*

4. *Swift County* (Minn.) *News,* August 29, 1967, p. 1.

5. *Swift County* (Minn.) *Monitor,* August 10, 1967, p. 1.

6. *Planning Reports* (Benson, Minn.: City Planning Commission and Midwest Planning and Research, August, 1961).

7. *Swift County* (Minn.) *Monitor,* October 6, 1966, p. 4.

8. *Ibid.,* p. 1.

9. According to Frank Wright, political reporter for the *Minneapolis Tribune* in his coverage of the campaign.

10. *Swift County* (Minn.) *Monitor,* August 18, 1966, p. 1, Section II.

11. *Ibid.,* August 25, 1966, p. 4.

12. *Ibid.,* September 1, 1966, p. 5.

13. *Swift County* (Minn.) *News,* September 6, 1966, p. 1.

14. *Swift County* (Minn.) *Monitor,* October 27, 1966, p. 1.

15. *Ibid.*

16. *Ibid.,* December 1, 1966, p. 1.

17. *Ibid.,* March 23, 1967, p. 1.

18. *Ibid.,* June 8, 1967, p. 1.

19. Max Weber, *From Max Weber,* trans. Hans Gerth and C. Wright Mills (New York: Oxford University Press, 1946), pp. 129 ff.

20. Floyd Hunter, *Community Power Structure* (New York: Doubleday, 1963), p. 181.

APPENDIXES

APPENDIX 1

THE
QUESTIONNAIRE

The questionnaire was put together only
after a preliminary review of the community
and on the basis of the application of the
theory to the findings. Where possible the
code numbers assigned for computer program-
ming are added in brackets. It is not possible
to indicate the coding on a few questions
where qualitative information was requested
or added by the respondents.

Part I: Social Characteristics of Bensonites

1. Check the age category in which you fall:
   1. 20 to 30 years of age _____ (7)
   2. 31 to 40 years of age _____ (5)
   3. 41 to 50 years of age _____ (3)
   4. 51 years of age and over _____ (1)

2. Check your schooling:
   1. Some grade school ＿＿＿＿＿＿＿＿ (1)
   2. Completed grade school ＿＿＿＿ (2)
   3. Some high school ＿＿＿＿＿＿＿＿ (3)
   4. Completed high school ＿＿＿＿ (4)
   5. Some college ＿＿＿＿＿＿＿＿＿＿ (5)
   6. Completed college ＿＿＿＿＿＿ (6)
   7. Hold graduate degrees ＿＿＿＿ (7)

3. Check your religious affiliation:
   1. Catholic ＿＿＿＿＿＿＿＿＿＿＿＿ (1)
   2. Protestant ＿＿＿＿＿＿＿＿＿＿ (7)
   3. Other, specify ＿＿＿＿＿＿＿＿ (7)

4. Check your marital status:
   1. Married ＿＿＿＿＿＿＿＿＿＿＿＿ (1)
   2. Unmarried ＿＿＿＿＿＿＿＿＿＿ (7)

5. Were your parents born in Benson?
   1. Yes ＿＿＿＿＿＿＿＿＿＿＿＿＿＿ (1)
   2. No ＿＿＿＿＿＿＿＿＿＿＿＿＿＿＿ (7)

6. Check your nationality:
   1. Norwegian ＿＿＿＿＿＿＿＿＿＿ (1)
   2. German ＿＿＿＿＿＿＿＿＿＿＿＿ (7)
   3. Other, specify ＿＿＿＿＿＿＿＿ (7)

7. What is your occupation?
   1. Farmer ＿＿＿＿＿＿＿＿＿＿＿＿ (1)
   2. Laborer ＿＿＿＿＿＿＿＿＿＿＿＿ (2)
   3. White-collar worker ＿＿＿＿ (3)
   4. Professional ＿＿＿＿＿＿＿＿＿ (4)
   5. Businessman ＿＿＿＿＿＿＿＿＿ (7)
   6. Other, specify ＿＿＿＿＿＿＿＿ (5)

8. Joint income:
   1. Under $5,000 per year ＿＿＿＿ (1)
   2. $5,000-7,999 per year ＿＿＿ (2)
   3. $8,000-9,999 per year ＿＿＿ (3)
   4. $10,000-11,999 per year ＿＿ (4)
   5. $12,000 and over per year ＿＿ (5)

SMALL TOWN AND THE NATION

9. If tools and/or equipment are used in your occupation, the value is:
   1. Under $100 _____ (1)
   2. $100-299 _____ (2)
   3. $300-499 _____ (3)
   4. $500-999 _____ (4)
   5. $1,000 and over _____ (5)

10. Are you currently on old-age assistance, retirement, or other pension?
    1. Yes _____ (1)
    2. No _____ (7)
    3. Other, specify _____ (7)

11. Ownership of business or other capital investment; value is:
    1. None _____ (1)
    2. Under $10,000 _____ (1)
    3. $10,000-29,999 _____ (3)
    4. $30,000-49,999 _____ (5)
    5. $50,000 and over _____ (7)

12. If house is owned, approximate present value is:
    1. Under $10,000 _____ (2)
    2. $10,000 to 14,999 _____ (3)
    3. $15,000 to 19,999 _____ (4)
    4. $20,000 to 29,999 _____ (5)
    5. $30,000 and over _____ (6)

13. Do you own or have you invested in any of the following properties?
    1. Boat (amount) _____
    2. Airplane (amount) _____
    3. Apartment (amount) _____
    4. House (amount) _____
    5. Store or warehouse (amount) _____
    6. Farm or land (amount) _____
       Acres _____
    7. Company (mfg., etc.) _____
       (amount) _____

14. How many cars do you own?
    1. None _____ (1)
    2. One car _____ (2)
    3. Two cars or more _____ (7)
    Year and make of each car _____

15. If you are a renter, what is the monthly rent?
    1. Under $55 _____ (2)
    2. $55 to 69 _____ (3)
    3. $70 to 84 _____ (4)
    4. $85 and over _____ (5)

16. Check the political party in which you have the greatest confidence:
    1. Republican party _____ (1)
    2. Democratic Party _____ (7)
    3. Other, specify _____ (7)

17. Check how often you attend the following:

	Regularly	Sometimes	Never
Benson Jaycees	____	____	____
Benson Lions	____	____	____
Benson Kiwanis	____	____	____
Chamber of Commerce	____	____	____
Farmers' Union	____	____	____
NFO	____	____	____
Farm Bureau	____	____	____
PTA	____	____	____
4-H Club	____	____	____
Church organization	____	____	____
Political party	____	____	____

18. Do you hold offices in above-specified organizations, or any other local organizations? If so, please specify your offices _____

_____

SMALL TOWN AND THE NATION

19. If you hold any office in any organization beyond the local level, please specify the office: _____

20. Do you have close friends who are active in either the Democratic or the Republican party in Benson?
    1. None _____ (1)
    2. One _____ (3)
    3. Two or more _____ (5)

21. How many close friends do you have among Benson's local elected officials?
    1. None _____ (1)
    2. 1 to 2 _____ (3)
    3. 3 to 4 _____ (5)
    4. 5 and over _____ (7)

22. Do you share hospitality (e.g., a house visit) with any of the following? Indicate how often in the appropriate box for each of these, such as: We have our pastor as house guest: never, sometimes, or often.

	Never	Sometimes	Often
1. Pastor	____	____	____
2. Doctor	____	____	____
3. Banker	____	____	____
4. Lawyer	____	____	____
5. Teacher	____	____	____
6. Judge	____	____	____

Part II. Questionnaire on Life and Society in Benson, Minn.

How do you feel about the following statements? Indicate for each one whether you strongly agree, agree, disagree, or strongly disagree. If you strongly agree, circle SA. If you

agree, circle A. If you disagree, circle D.
If you strongly disagree, circle SD. Do so for
each of the following statements:

23. Youngsters do not respect their elders
    enough nowadays.
    SA (1)   A (3)   D (5)   SD (7)

24. The primary objective of education should
    be to adjust the individual to a happy
    life in Benson.
    SA (1)   A (3)   D (5)   SD (7)

25. Knowing Benson's history and traditions
    is an important lesson which youngsters
    should learn.
    SA (1)   A (3)   D (5)   SD (7)

26. Education should prepare the individual
    for the outside world.
    SA (7)   A (5)   D (3)   SD (1)

27. Youngsters in school should read whatever
    books they wish.
    SA (7)   A (5)   D (3)   SD (1)

28. Too few of the young people plan on
    remaining in Benson.
    SA (1)   A (3)   D (5)   SD (7)

29. To be really educated one should study in
    Europe for a while.
    SA (7)   A (5)   D (3)   SD (1)

30. Religion is essential to a successful and
    happy life.
    SA (1)   A (3)   D (5)   SD (7)

31. There are persons in Benson who think that
    religion is not necessary for happiness.
    SA (7)   A (5)   D (3)   SD (1)

32. People should stay true to the religion they were raised in.
    SA (1)   A (3)   D (5)   SD (7)

33. Marriages between people of different religions don't work.
    SA (1)   A (3)   D (5)   SD (7)

34. Marriages between families in the same social level work best.
    SA (1)   A (3)   D (5)   SD (7)

35. The rest of one's family ought to have some say in the choice of one's marriage partner.
    SA (1)   A (3)   D (5)   SD (7)

36. Divorce ruins a person's chances for another happy marriage.
    SA (1)   A (3)   D (5)   SD (7)

37. The control of local Benson businesses by outsiders is not a bad thing.
    SA (7)   A (5)   D (3)   SD (1)

38. People living in Benson should patronize Benson businesses to keep the money in Benson.
    SA (1)   A (3)   D (5)   SD (7)

39. It will be a good thing for America when big corporations own all the farms.
    SA (7)   A (5)   D (3)   SD (1)

40. Benson's firms should be locally owned if at all possible.
    SA (1)   A (3)   D (5)   SD (7)

41. The small family farm is the backbone of the nation.
    SA (1)   A (3)   D (5)   SD (7)

42. Most workers in Benson are underpaid.
    SA (1)   A (3)   D (5)   SD (7)

43. Small towns like Benson should be able
    to get money from the government for rural
    renewal just like big cities get money
    for urban renewal.
    SA (1)   A (3)   D (5)   SD (7)

44. Government is best that does the least,
    and the federal government should keep
    itself out of our business as much as
    possible.
    SA (1)   A (3)   D (5)   SD (7)

45. When a son has his father's homestead, he
    should do all he can to keep that family
    farm in the family name.
    SA (1)   A (3)   D (5)   SD (7)

46. It would be a good thing for Benson if
    many farmers sold out their land for
    wildlife refuges and other such uses.
    SA (7)   A (5)   D (3)   SD (1)

47. The most important source of wealth is
    land.
    SA (1)   A (3)   D (5)   SD (7)

48. The more land a man can own the better off
    he is.
    SA (1)   A (3)   D (5)   SD (7)

49. Big government has too much power these
    days, and more power should be kept at the
    local level.
    SA (1)   A (3)   D (5)   SD (7)

50. Reapportionment did the right thing in
    taking power away from rural areas and
    giving more power to cities because
    cities have more people nowadays.
    SA (7)   A (5)   D (3)   SD (1)

SMALL TOWN AND THE NATION

51. Government is best that does the least.
    SA (1)   A (3)   D (5)   SD (7)

52. Farmers will be at the mercy of big-city markets until the farmers use collective bargaining just like labor unions did in the big cities.
    SA (7)   A (5)   D (3)   SD (1)

53. Farmers are not paid enough for their products.
    SA (1)   A (3)   D (5)   SD (7)

54. The NFO (National Farmers Organization) is doing a real service for America.
    SA (7)   A (5)   D (3)   SD (1)

55. Civic groups should try harder to get more industry into Benson.
    SA (1)   A (3)   D (5)   SD (7)

56. The only way you can influence local government in Benson is by voting.
    SA (1)   A (3)   D (5)   SD (7)

57. Local politics in Benson is too complicated for me to know what is going on.
    SA (1)   A (3)   D (5)   SD (7)

58. Parking meters are a good thing for Benson.
    SA (7)   A (5)   D (3)   SD (1)

59. Local political officials in Benson do not care much about what I think.
    SA (1)   A (3)   D (5)   SD (7)

60. The old, prominent families in Benson still have a lot to say about what happens in Benson.
    SA (1)   A (3)   D (5)   SD (7)

Appendixes

61. Nowadays it is newcomers to Benson who get things done in local politics.
    SA (7)   A (5)   D (3)   SD (1)

62. Even if he is happier in Benson, a man should leave Benson if he gets a much better-paying job in a big city.
    SA (7)   A (5)   D (3)   SD (1)

63. There are good points to life in Benson that money cannot buy.
    SA (1)   A (3)   D (5)   SD (7)

64. A small town like Benson is the best place in the world to rear a family.
    SA (1)   A (3)   D (5)   SD (7)

65. Life in a small town like Benson is generally more wholesome than life in a big city.
    SA (1)   A (3)   D (5)   SD (7)

SMALL TOWN AND THE NATION

APPENDIX 2

METHODOLOGICAL APPENDIX

No study of the dynamics of community change can conceivably be complete that omits a historical review. Rich resources of material were available for the historical phases of the present study. Since it is the hometown of one of the present writers, the participant-observation experiences of his entire life were available for interpretation of findings. Collections of old newspapers were available extending through almost the entire history of the community. For demographic data, the ten-year federal census was consulted. Of especial value was the rich collection of materials in the Swift County Historical Society. These were generously made available to the researchers. The history of Swift County, reconstructed by Stanley Holte Anonsen, is one of the primary sources in the establishment of such basic themes as the period of the Indians, the first white settlement, and the period of Benson's founding fathers. Although Anonsen's focus is far wider than Benson, his published history offered an invaluable check on folklore.[1]

Since the concern of the study was directed primarily to the isolation of various life-strategies arising in response to attempts in Benson to maintain local community autonomy on the one hand and to adapt to the forces of the wider world on the other, an analytical survey seemed indicated. Interest centered on the contrasts and tensions between those oriented to the autonomy of the locality and those receptive to various outside interests.

A series of hypotheses were advanced with respect to differences in social condition and in attitudes between three categories of Bensonites: those Bensonites oriented toward the old autonomous town, old-style Bensonites; those Bensonites oriented toward the various translocal forces that play upon Benson, new-style Bensonites; and those persons who by choice or necessity have made their ways into the wider society, the ex-Bensonites.

Since the primary focus of study is on various hypothesized contrasts between old-style and new-style Bensonites, random samples were drawn of these two groups. An additional sample was drawn of ex-Bensonites. The ex-Bensonites, in effect, function as a "control" with respect to the study of old- and new-style Bensonites. If ex-Bensonites did not show some displacement both in social characteristics and attitudes which brings them nearer to the members of the wider society than old-style Bensonites, something would indeed be wrong. Three-way comparisons are suggested by this grouping:

188

old-style Bensonites *versus* new-style Bensonites
old-style Bensonites *versus* ex-Bensonites
new-style Bensonites *versus* ex-Bensonites

The primary comparisons were between old-style Bensonites and new-style Bensonites, and between old-style Bensonites and ex-Bensonites. Since new-style Bensonites and ex-Bensonites were theorized to be alike, only random differences were expected between them.

THE INSTRUMENT

The basic instrument for gathering data was a self-administered questionnaire covering a variety of characteristics deemed relevant to localism and cosmopolitanism, respectively. Moreover, an important division of the questionnaire consisted of a series of attitude-opinion statements, the responses to which were theorized to reveal differences in innercommunity or extracommunity orientation. Such attitude-opinion statements had four possible response categories, from Strongly Agree to Strongly Disagree. For example, a given statement might read as follows:

> The primary objective of education should be to adjust the individual to a happy life in Benson.
> 1) Strongly   2) Agree   3) Disagree   4) Strongly
>   Agree   Disagree

One could theorize that old-style Bensonites would be more

inclined to the Agree end of the scale than the new-style Bensonites or ex-Bensonites. If one assigns the scale numbers 1, 2, 3, 4 to the response categories Strongly Agree, Agree, Disagree, Strongly Disagree, respectively, responses to this statement form a crude attitude scale. The higher the score an individual receives, the greater his tendency toward the "cosmopolitan" end of the scale. One's hypotheses now assume the specific form of anticipating that new-style Bensonites and ex-Bensonites will obtain higher scores on the cosmopolitan end of the scale than old-style Bensonites.

Reliability of the Instrument

The instrument was revised at least five times in consultation with various experts and with members of the Benson community. To test the reliability of the instrument it was administered to the members of a seminar on February 13, 1967, and again to the same members of the seminar on February 27, 1967. The degree of association between the two sets of scores was calculated by the Spearman rank correlation coefficient[2] and found well within acceptable limits.

Validity of the Instrument

Two basic methods were employed to determine the validity of the instrument and the various scales: (1) the method of known groups and (2) the method of jury opinion.[3] Known old-style Bensonites, known new-style Bensonites, and known ex-Bensonites were given the questionnaire, and comparisons were made between the response and the theoretically predicted results. The following results were obtained.

190

TABLE 47

COMPARISON OF PRETEST RESPONSES
TO A SELECTED SERIES OF QUESTIONS:
KNOWN OLD- AND NEW-STYLE BENSONITES

QUESTION DESIGNATION	Average New-Style	Average Old-Style	Validation Judgment
2	3.25	2.6	plus
3	2.25	2.0	plus
4	3.5	1.8	plus
10	2.5	1.8	plus
11	2.75	1.8	plus
13	3.25	2.2	plus
14	3.0	2.0	plus
15	2.25	1.0	plus

TABLE 48

COMPARISON OF PRETEST RESPONSES
TO A SELECTED SERIES OF QUESTIONS:
KNOWN EX-BENSONITES AND KNOWN OLD-STYLE BENSONITES

QUESTION DESIGNATION	Average Ex-Bensonites	Average Old-Style	Validation Judgment
2	3.6	2.6	plus
3	2.2	2.0	plus
4	3.5	1.8	plus
10	2.75	1.8	plus
11	2.5	1.8	plus
13	3.0	2.2	plus
14	3.25	2.0	plus
15	2.0	1.0	plus

TABLE 49

COMPARISON OF PRE-TEST RESPONSES
TO A SELECTED SERIES OF QUESTIONS:
KNOWN EX-BENSONITES AND KNOWN NEW-STYLE BENSONITES

QUESTION DESIGNATION	Average Ex-Bensonites	Average New-Style	Validation Judgment
2	3.6	3.25	plus
3	2.2	2.25	plus
4	3.5	3.5	plus
10	2.75	2.5	plus
11	2.5	2.75	plus
13	3.0	3.25	plus
14	3.25	3.0	plus
15	2.0	2.25	plus

Known Groups

Rather than reproduce the entire results, a sample of the findings are reported here. Test groups of known old-style Bensonites, known new-style Bensonites, and known ex-Bensonites were given a sample of questions in a test and retest process, and these were the average scores on those questionnaires. A plus indicates whether scores varied in the predicted direction.

As anticipated with ex-Bensonites and new-style Bensonites, no systematic differences appeared between them.

1. Stanley Holte Anonsen, *A History of Swift County* (Benson, Minn.: Swift County Historical Society, 1929).

2. Sidney Siegel, *Nonparametric Statistics for the Behavioral Sciences* (New York: McGraw-Hill, 1956), pp. 202–210.

3. Claire Sellitz, *Research Methods in Social Relations* (New York: Holt, Rinehart and Winston, 1961), pp. 155–166.

APPENDIX 3

STATISTICAL
APPENDIX

At the time a sample of the ex-Bensonites was drawn, the possibility was considered that the degree of cosmopolitanism they displayed might possibly be different depending on whether they migrated to some large metropolitan center or to a small town such as Benson. To keep control over this possibility, the group of ex-Bensonites was originally divided into two: ex-Bensonite metropolitans and ex-Bensonite locals. Hence when mean scores were originally calculated, there were four sets of findings: old-style Bensonites, new-style Bensonites, ex-Bensonite metropolitans, and ex-Bensonite locals. The findings on the sixty-five items of the questionnaire are shown in Table 50.

In traits (the first twenty-two items), the two subgroups of ex-Bensonites were quite similar. If there was a selective factor that led ex-Bensonites to make their way in large cos-

TABLE 50

MEAN SCORES BY ITEM OF ALL SAMPLE GROUPS

QUESTIONNAIRE ITEM	Old-Style Bensonites	New-Style Bensonites	Ex-Bensonite Metropolitans	Ex-Bensonite Locals
1	2.00	4.13	3.44	3.35
2	4.23	4.78	5.27	5.11
3	6.05	6.51	7.00	6.64
4	1.63	1.00	3.66	1.70
5	5.73	6.51	5.00	5.23
6	3.36	5.37	3.66	4.17
7	3.60	5.21	4.50	3.94
8	2.81	2.86	2.72	2.82
9	3.65	3.29	3.44	3.58
10	5.73	7.00	6.00	6.64
11	2.68	1.70	1.77	2.76
12	3.18	2.64	3.05	2.47
13	2.34	2.35	2.61	2.11
14	3.60	3.43	3.27	3.70
15	1.13	1.81	1.38	1.52
16	3.68	2.94	3.00	3.47
17	3.10	3.27	2.77	3.64
18	1.94	1.91	1.55	1.70
19	1.52	1.21	1.00	1.11
20	3.36	3.91	2.11	3.47
21	3.21	3.64	2.22	1.94
22	5.07	5.32	4.55	5.11
23	2.94	3.43	3.11	3.23
24	3.78	5.21	4.55	4.00
25	2.94	3.48	3.55	3.00
26	6.15	6.24	6.22	6.52
27	2.84	3.05	3.44	3.11
28	2.89	3.32	3.55	2.88
29	2.63	2.51	2.88	2.52
30	1.84	1.86	1.44	1.94
31	4.84	5.00	5.11	4.64
32	3.36	4.35	3.66	3.58

TABLE 50 (continued)

QUESTIONNAIRE ITEM	Old-Style Bensonites	New-Style Bensonites	Ex-Bensonite Metropolitans	Ex-Bensonite Locals
33	3.84	4.89	3.88	3.47
34	2.94	3.16	2.77	3.47
35	4.68	5.05	5.00	4.88
36	4.21	5.00	5.00	4.29
37	3.15	4.13	3.88	2.88
38	2.47	2.62	2.77	2.29
39	1.73	1.81	1.77	1.47
40	2.26	2.62	2.77	2.52
41	2.47	3.48	3.66	2.64
42	2.89	2.62	3.33	2.88
43	2.78	3.27	3.22	3.70
44	3.84	3.54	3.55	3.11
45	3.10	3.70	3.44	3.47
46	2.42	2.62	2.77	2.05
47	2.94	3.10	3.33	5.00
48	4.42	4.18	3.88	4.64
49	2.68	3.10	3.11	2.41
50	2.84	3.43	3.44	2.64
51	4.84	4.56	5.22	4.41
52	4.84	4.62	4.33	4.64
53	2.89	2.51	2.77	2.17
54	3.26	3.81	3.33	4.05
55	2.63	2.78	2.33	3.11
56	3.31	4.13	3.66	3.47
57	4.52	5.48	5.11	5.11
58	3.57	4.24	4.44	3.00
59	3.52	4.62	4.11	4.64
60	4.89	4.24	4.00	4.64
61	3.42	3.75	4.11	3.58
62	3.57	3.48	3.77	4.29
63	2.52	2.51	2.66	3.47
64	2.52	2.94	3.66	3.11
65	2.10	2.18	2.88	2.64

SMALL TOWN AND THE NATION

mopolitan centers rather than in small towns like their own it does not appear. In attitudes, the two subgroups of ex-Bensonites were fairly similar with, however, some twenty out of thirty-three attitude items falling in the expected direction. The contrast between the two subgroups of ex-Bensonites was not great enough to warrant keeping them separate. For purposes of comparison with Bensonites, the sub-samples of ex-Bensonites were collapsed.

Chi-square comparisons were run on the two groups of Bensonites and the ex-Bensonites; the findings are summarized in Tables 51 and 52.

The rather confused picture that results when Benson-

TABLE 51

OLD-STYLE AND EX-BENSONITES
COMPARED BY TRAITS AND ATTITUDES

	Not Found Significant	Found Significant
Traits	11	11
Attitudes	21	22

TABLE 52

NEW-STYLE AND EX-BENSONITES
COMPARED BY TRAITS AND ATTITUDES

	Not Found Significant	Found Significant
Traits	6	16
Attitudes	24	19

TABLE 53

CHI-SQUARE COMPARISONS OF BENSONITES AND EX-BENSONITES

QUESTIONNAIRE ITEM	Old-Style Bensonites— Ex-Bensonites	Significance[a]	New-Style Bensonites— Ex-Bensonites	Significance[a]
1	3.25	NS	9.14	.01
2	7.81	.01	4.86	.05
3	1.74	NS	3.77	.05
4	6.45	.01	1.58	NS[b]
5	4.36	.05	3.93	.05
6	3.88	.05	3.11	NS
7	1.21	NS	3.21	NS
8	1.04	NS	3.73	.05
9	8.18	.01	3.09	NS
10	6.15	.01	3.69	.05
11	3.07	NS	6.96	.01
12	5.11	.05	2.90	NS
13	1.81	NS	4.22	.05
14	3.06	NS	2.78	NS
15	8.02	.01	8.26	.01
16	2.69	NS	5.73	.02
17	9.43	.01	7.25	.01
18	3.60	.05	6.96	.01
19	2.86	NS	5.62	.02
20	2.13	NS	5.27	.02
21	1.35	NS	8.76	.01
22	4.15	.05	9.09	.01
23	4.36	.05	2.78	NS
24	4.01	.05	1.58	NS
25	2.91	NS	2.78	NS
26	3.88	.05	4.86	.05
27	1.92	NS	1.19	NS
28	2.10	NS	1.45	NS
29	2.48	NS	1.20	NS
30	1.32	NS	4.37	.05
31	4.67	.05	1.85	NS
32	6.30	.02	2.41	NS

198

TABLE 53 (continued)

QUESTIONNAIRE ITEM	Old-Style Bensonites— Ex-Bensonites	Significance[a]	New-Style Bensonites— Ex-Bensonites	Significance[a]
33	8.18	.01	1.58	NS
34	3.48	NS	2.38	NS
35	4.31	.05	5.16	.05
36	1.96	NS	2.44	NS
37	7.08	.01	5.62	.02
38	1.65	NS	6.96	.01
39	5.63	.02	7.37	.01
40	6.20	.02	2.91	NS
41	5.32	.02	7.37	.01
42	2.59	NS	1.40	NS
43	2.23	NS	5.16	.02
44	1.53	NS	4.22	.05
45	1.56	NS	5.73	.02
46	6.20	.02	2.75	NS
47	4.36	.05	7.09	.01
48	1.96	NS	2.52	NS
49	2.11	NS	2.86	NS
50	2.84	NS	5.73	.02
51	9.36	.01	1.88	NS
52	7.38	.01	6.39	.02
53	4.55	.05	8.26	.01
54	4.93	.05	6.59	.02
55	4.36	.05	3.66	NS
56	4.93	.05	9.09	.01
57	4.36	.05	2.91	NS
58	1.21	NS	3.90	.05
59	1.08	NS	6.39	.02
60	2.09	NS	3.21	NS
61	1.50	NS	5.78	.02
62	6.30	.02	3.39	NS
63	4.36	.05	2.60	NS
64	1.74	NS	2.79	NS
65	3.05	NS	2.69	NS

[a] At one degree of freedom.   [b] NS = not significant.

ites are compared to ex-Bensonites seems to result as much from the fact that, in general, the ex-Bensonites are more cosmopolitan than old-style Bensonites and somewhat less cosmopolitan in many respects than new-style Bensonites. The complete summary of findings is listed in Table 53.

BIBLIOGRAPHY

Adams, Henry. *History of the United States.* Vol. 1. New York: Scribners, 1889.

Anfinson, Ronald. *Swift County* (Minn.) *Monitor.* Editorial reprinted in *Minneapolis Tribune,* July 7, 1967.

Anonsen, Stanley Holte. *A History of Swift County.* Benson, Minn.: Swift County Historical Society, 1929.

Folwell, William Watts. *History of Minnesota.* Vol. 1. Saint Paul: Minnesota Historical Society, 1921.

Galpin, C. J. *The Social Anatomy of an Agricultural Village.* Research Bulletin, no. 34. Madison, Wis.: Agricultural Experiment Station of the University of Wisconsin, 1915.

Gerth, Hans, and Mills, C. Wright. *Character and Social Structure.* New York: Harcourt Brace, 1953.

Herfindahl, Lewis. "Tribute No. 26." In *Floyd B. Olson: Minnesota's Greatest Liberal Governor, A Memorial Volume,* edited by John S. McGrath and James J. Delmont. Saint Paul: McGrath and Delmont, 1937.

Hunter, Floyd. *Community Power Structure.* New York: Doubleday, 1963.

Iverson, Noel. "Germania, U.S.A.: The Dynamics of Change of an Ethnic Community into a Status Community." Minneapolis: Ph.D. dissertation, University of Minnesota, 1964.

Langlois, Charles V., and Seignobos, Charles. *Introduction to the Study of History.* New York: Henry Holt, 1925.

Light and Life. Benson, Minn.: Our Redeemer's Lutheran Church, 1967.

Lindeman, E. C. "Community." In *Encyclopedia of the Social Sciences.* New York: Macmillan, 1934.

Lyford, Joseph B. *The Talk in Vandalia.* Charlotte, N.C.: McNally and Loftin, 1962.

MacIver, R. M. *Community.* New York: Macmillan, 1917.

Maine, Henry Sumner. New York: Henry Holt, 1906.

Martindale, Don. *American Social Structure.* New York: Appleton-Century-Crofts, 1960.

———. *American Society.* New York: D. Van Nostrand, 1960.

———. *The Nature and Types of Sociological Theory.* Boston: Houghton Mifflin, 1960.

———. *Social Life and Cultural Change.* New York: D. Van Nostrand, 1962.

——— and Monachesi, Elio D. *Elements of Sociology.* New York: Harper and Brothers, 1951.

Minneapolis Tribune, August 18, 1967.

Minnesota Executive Documents, 1876. Vol. 1. Saint Paul: Minnesota Historical Society, 1876.

SMALL TOWN AND THE NATION

Minor, John. In *West Central* (Willmar, Minn.) *Tribune,* April 28, 1967. "Letters to the Editor."

Park, Robert E.; Burgess, Ernest W. and McKenzie, Roderick. *The City.* Chicago: University of Chicago Press, 1925.

Paxson, F. L. *History of the American Frontier.* Boston: Houghton Mifflin, 1924.

"Philosophy of the Benson Public Schools." Mimeographed. Benson, Minn.: Benson Public School System, n.d.

Planning Reports. Benson, Minn.: City Planning Commission and Midwest Planning and Research, August, 1961.

Pond, S. W. *Two Volunteers Among the Dakotas.* Boston: Congregationalist Sunday School Publishing Society, 1893.

Schlesinger, Arthur. "History: Mistress and Handmaiden." In *Essays on Research in the Social Sciences.* Washington, D.C.: The Brookings Institution Committee on Training, 1949.

Sellitz, Claire. *Research Methods in Social Relations.* New York: Holt, Rinehart and Winston, 1961.

Siegel, Sidney. *Nonparametric Statistics for the Behavioral Sciences.* New York: McGraw-Hill, 1956.

Stein, Maurice R. *The Eclipse of Community.* Princeton, N.J.: Princeton University Press, 1960.

Steiner, J. F. *The American Community in Action.* New York: Henry Holt, 1928.

Swift County (Minn.) *Monitor,* August 18, 1966; August 25. 1966; August 26, 1966; September 1, 1966; September 6, 1966; October 6, 1966; October 27, 1966; December 1, 1966; January 12, 1967; March 23, 1967; June 8, 1967; June 17, 1967; July 6, 1967; July 27, 1967; August 10, 1967; August 17, 1967; August 29, 1967.

Swift County (Minn.) *News,* August 29, 1967; October 11, 1967.

Toennies, Ferdinand. *Gemeinschaft und Gesellschaft*. Leipzig: K. Curtius, 1887.

Vidich, Arthur J., and Bensman, Joseph. *Small Town in Mass Society*. New York: Doubleday Anchor Books, 1960.

Warner, W. Lloyd. *Democracy in Jonesville*. New York: Harper and Brothers, 1949.

Weber, Max. *From Max Weber*. Translated by Hans Gerth and C. Wright Mills. New York: Oxford University Press, 1946.

West Central (Willmar, Minn.) *Tribune,* August 14, 1967; August 18, 1967.

West, James. *Plainville, U.S.A.* New York: Columbia University Press, 1945.

Winchell, N. H. *The Aborigines of Minnesota*. Saint Paul: St. Paul Pioneer Press Co., 1911.

Winchell, N. H., and Upham, Warren. *The Geology of Minnesota*. Vol. 2. Saint Paul: St. Paul Pioneer Press Co., Printers, 1889.

Wright, Frank. *Minneapolis Tribune* coverage of the 1966 Congressional campaign in Minnesota's Sixth Congressional District.

Yearbook, 1949–1950, Swift County-Benson Hospital Auxiliary. Benson, Minn.: privately printed, 1949.

Young, Pauline V., and Schmic, Calvin F. *Scientific Social Surveys and Research*. Englewood Cliffs, N.J.: Prentice-Hall, 1956.

SMALL TOWN AND THE NATION

INDEX

SMALL TOWN AND THE NATION

208
———

209

Index

Index